Nothing Good Ever Happens to Me:
An Adoption Love Story

NOTHING

AN

GOOD

ADOPTION

EVER

LOVE

HAPPENS

STORY

Caroline Hassinger Lindsay

TO ME

Child & Family Press
Washington, DC

Child & Family Press
is an imprint of the Child Welfare League of America, Inc.

CHILD WELFARE LEAGUE OF AMERICA, INC.
440 First Street, NW, Suite 310, Washington, DC 20001-2085

CURRENT PRINTING (last digit)
10 9 8 7 6 5 4 3 2 1

Cover design by James Graham
Text design by Jennifer M. Price

Printed in the United States of America

ISBN # 0–87868–601–0

Library of Congress Cataloging-in-Publication Data
Lindsay, Caroline Hassinger, 1931-
    Nothing good ever happens to me : an adoption love story /
Caroline Hassinger Lindsay.
        p.   cm.
    ISBN 0-87868-601-0 (pbk.)
    1. Older child adoption--United States--Case studies. 2. Adopted
children--United States--Family relationships--Case studies.
3. Foster children--United States--Case studies.   I. Title.
HV875.55.L545 1996
362.7'34--dc20   96-12010

To my daughter herein called Leigh/Lee Ann,
to my sons Stephen and Tim and my daughter Susan,
to my husband Paul,
and to my father Martin Hassinger

Contents

Acknowledgments

I would like to acknowledge the help of several people who especially made this project possible.

First, to my daughter, in this book called Leigh/Lee Ann: for being so willing to share her story in the hope of helping some other child in a similar situation; for her encouragement by reading the manuscript in each of its many stages, to see if my memories were similar to her own; and for all that I learned from her about children, families, and the richness of life in the living of this story.

To my other three children, Stephen, Tim, and Susan: for their participation and reflection upon our life together and their willingness for me to share these events, which are also their story.

To my husband, Paul: for the insights, appreciation, and search for our mutual understanding of the experiences we had shared; for his encouragement throughout the writing; for his many helpful suggestions; and for all of the word processing it took to get this into a usable form.

To my father, Martin Hassinger: not only for living this experience with us with loving support and sensitivity, but also for his persistent belief that there are many people "who need this book."

And to Ruth Smullin, who believed in this project from the time we met in a writer's group: for sharing her expertise as an editor to help me order and organize the material, for her sensitive understanding of the feelings of children in difficult situations, and for her warm friendship and encouragement to complete this manuscript.

To Susan Brite and Mary Liepold at the Child Welfare League of America: for their appreciation of this story, their belief that it will be valuable to adoptive parents, and their skillful work in bringing it to publication.

There are many others who read drafts of this work and gave suggestions and encouragement. They are too numerous to mention by name, but I appreciate their help.

Some of the names of the people and places in this story have been changed.

Prologue

This is the story of events that happened in our family from the time Leigh came to live with us in 1958 as a seven-year-old foster child until her legal adoption into our family 10 years later.

A few years after this story ends, I made a scrapbook, collecting photos and filling the pages with paragraphs of memories of the first 10 years we spent together. My purpose in doing this was to present Leigh with what I hoped was a balanced view of our life at that time. It seemed to me that she thought of herself only in terms of her problems: the difficulties in school, the tantrums, the poor relationships with other children. But I wanted her also to remember the little girl who absorbed new experiences and information eagerly, assessed her situation and the people around her with blunt honesty, and charmed everyone with her lively sense of humor. She was a survivor who took a chance on life.

In the years that followed, friends who knew about our experiences introduced me to their friends who were in situations similar to ours. I believe that hearing our story was helpful to them. As I told our story and listened to others', I became aware of common themes in the lives of adoptive families. I wanted to share what I had learned in a form that would be useful to families adopting older children or taking in foster children, as well as to social workers or lawyers, whose decisions might be informed by a personal experience.

In raising a foster or adopted child, as in raising any child, there is no guidebook or road map to a successful outcome. We soon discovered that if we tried a lot of different things, we could assess what worked, go with that, and discard the ideas that failed. I began to think of it this way: If you try 100 things and 90 fail, you have 10 successes.

Any definition of success that we previously held or that society held had to be revised. We adopted the philosophy that success is best defined as movement in a positive direction. Expecting to achieve certain things by certain times did not work.

We received a lot of advice about our daughter, and it came from opposite points of view. Some people said, "This child has never had enough structure to count on. You need to be very strict." Others said, "Poor thing, she has had such a hard life. You mustn't expect too much of her." Neither approach seemed right to us, so we developed our own ideas. We expected a lot of her and tried to state this clearly, but when it didn't work out, we would try to find out why and renegotiate. A kaleidoscope is a useful image to explain this flexible process. What we did was not like a stained glass window, static and unmoving; nor was it like a bowl full of broken colored glass pieces with no form. Instead, it resembled translucent glass held in place by a movable structure to make an infinite number of patterns.

We also had to think in new terms about what it means to be family. In our family, in addition to Leigh, we have two sons adopted as infants and a daughter who was born to us. In the kind of family we are conditioned to think of as "normal," the parents and children share genetic ties, and it's easy to know what to write on the pediatrician's medical history form. A certain trait in a child reminds us of Great-Uncle Henry, and if there is musical talent, we think we know where it came from.

In families constituted by adoption, the legal ties are firm, ensuring the future from the time the adoption becomes final. Family medical history may be scarce, and information often stops at the time the child is placed for adoption. Because the family doesn't share genetic ties, parents can deal for a child's lifetime with the frustrating aspects of unsuspected diseases or conditions that may have been inherited or influenced by prenatal experience. The family will also be enriched by traits and talents that appear unexpectedly in the child.

One way our families are different is the existence of birth parents in the adopted child's past. It is now commonly accepted that children need to be told the story of their adoption in a way that is appropriate to their stage of development. It is also important to work through the feelings around this information. At the beginning, the story told to the child is about the joy the adoptive parents knew in finding the child and the "chosenness" of their relationship. When the child is a little older, the existence of other parents becomes clear. The birth parents' reasons for placing the child for adoption become part of the story.

At this point many children have feelings of rejection. The child wonders if something is wrong with him that made his "first parents" not want to keep him. Answering the child's questions is easier if there is enough information about why the birth parents could not care for her or him to give an honest and sympathetic explanation.

The child may accept the idea that the biological parents could not take care of her and made a loving decision to find a family that could. But this raises an additional problem. If one family loved her and couldn't care for her, could this happen again? Some children develop fears of abandonment. It helps the child if we share the circumstances of our life that make it unlikely to happen: good health and strong commitment, for example. For one of my children, it helped to look at my will and to read the arrangements that we had made for the care of our children.

These feelings and others that children may have are not worked through only once, but again and again in different forms at every stage of development and in every life crisis. For example, the feelings of rejection often reappear in adopted adults when they become parents. The baby may be the first genetically connected relative in the adopted person's life. The intensity of the feelings surrounding the birth of a child once again raises the question: How could my biological parent have had this experience and made the decision that we would not be together? Intense experiences in adult life sometimes bring a desire to hear the story of the adoption decision told by the people who lived it.

One of my children made contact with his biological family. The experience confirmed the story we had told him and answered many questions about circumstances in the family at the time of his birth. He also received some crucial medical and genetic information. We all met, and it was a healing experience for the first family, the adoptive family, and the adopted adult.

In addition to working through the feelings of the adopted child, the adoptive parents have feelings of their own to work through. For the adoptive parents, there are the reasons for adoption. Although there are many adoptions where infertility is not a factor, sometimes there is great sadness about not being able to give birth to children. Sometimes there is also a sense of failure. There can be great frustration over infertility testing and perhaps unsuccessful treatment. All of these things need to be worked through to a comfortable level.

In the case of older children there is the remembered past, the other people in their lives—parents they may have lived with, siblings they may miss very much, foster families they felt close to. Even in cases where there has been abuse or serious neglect, children feel strong ties and a sadness at breaking these relationships. All of the child's early experiences affect the everyday life of the adoptive family. At times adoptive parents may feel frustrated at having to deal with the child's anger when that anger was caused by past events in which they were not involved and which they do not necessarily understand.

Family foster care or temporary care presents different problems. Sometimes it is unclear which decisions the parents can make and which will be made by other people. The child has no past that she shares with her foster family, nor is she assured of a future with them. There are often other people in the present time who she does have to deal with—biological relatives, social workers, siblings. What can parents do with all this?

In our case, we shared our own history, extended family, childhood memories, and family values—these became the shared past for all of our children. We built up memories and traditions; we had family celebrations. We developed a lot of shared experience—places we went, things we regularly did, things we all thought were funny or sad. We had pets and tree houses and special family meals.

We defined our family by its genetic and legal ties, but most importantly, by emotional ties—of caring and commitment and being a safe place where each person could share his or her deepest values and concerns. For Leigh, though we could not assure the future, we made sure we did nothing to make it less predictable. We arranged our life so she could stay with us and we did everything we could to make her adoption possible. In the meantime, she was a full member of the family and in no way did our commitment depend on her behavior.

Many older children who are adopted or come into foster care have had such harsh disappointments in life—including outright deception by adults—that they trust no one and nothing that is said or promised. It takes a long time to change this. Parents have to be committed truth tellers. I can remember Leigh asking me, sometimes in words and sometimes only with her eyes, "Do you really believe what you just said?" I would have to search deep into myself for the answer, because I was aware that she was staking her future trust in people on my ability to give straight answers. It was not enough to tell her she couldn't do something because the neighbors wouldn't approve. I had to find out whether I approved. The things we planned really had to happen, unless, of course, illness or other understandable things required changes.

Because life has been so uncontrollable, so unpredictable for these children, they often cling to black-and-white interpretations of things. Simplicity feels safe. But life doesn't work that way, and children must be helped to live with ambivalence. I am indebted to my father for something he told us over and over as I was growing up: "Nothing is as good as we think it will be or as bad." And I thank an adoptive mother of several older children, who often said, "Bring me 16 possible solutions, then we'll talk about the problem." My children call the talking about choices "Mother's Lecture on Keeping Your Options Open." Sometimes a problem needs to be discussed outright, but more often the door of the mind can be pushed open a little with subtle statements and questions, like, "Well, maybe not," "Is that always the answer?" and "What else could have happened?"

Paul and I read books on child development. We talked to social workers and psychotherapists. We got all the help we could, but the most helpful thing was concentrating on the child herself. We knew our child was unique. We learned to work with her and to understand her by relating to her, watching, listening to see who she was and who she might become.

We found that no matter how well we parented, how much we loved, the past could not be fixed. The first bonding had been broken; the devastating things had happened. We could listen, and we could add happy times and successful relationships, but we could not make the sadness disappear. What we could do, over a very long time and with much effort, was remove the sadness from the center—where it felt like the only thing in her life—to the edges. It was still there and needing to be worked out again at every new stage of development and each life crisis, but now it was only one of many things in her life.

These themes are, of course, important to all parenting, relating, and teaching. But to a child in the impermanent and insecure place of needing foster care or adoption, the margin of safety is very narrow. Being understood as an individual who is competent, valuable, and lovable is the only means of survival.

Part 1

The phone rang. It was Peg, a social worker from Neighborhood House, a private agency about an hour and a half away. We had sought their help for some children with whom we were working. The agency also had agreed to accept our application to adopt a baby, though they had none to place at that time.

The social worker had been talking to us about foster placement. I told her that we weren't ready to think about foster care at this point. She wanted us to consider taking a little boy who had been in a treatment center for children and needed a brief temporary placement until he could go home. Although I told her we were sure we didn't want a child we could not adopt, Peg encouraged us to consider it.

As I hung up the phone, I saw the stack of mail on the desk. There was a letter from an infertility specialist we were seeing in New York telling us it was time to apply for adoption. A letter from our state Welfare Department informed us that no state adoption agencies existed in our part of the state and urged us to work for social change. A letter from the Lutheran Children's Home expressed regrets, since they placed children only with Lutheran families. I slammed the desk closed.

Paul and I were both 26 and we had been married for three years. We had wanted to have a baby right away, and had first consulted the infertility specialist 18 months before. She was not able to help us, so for the past six months we had investigated every avenue of adoption. All adoptions in our community were arranged by a county probation officer, whose only qualification was that he was the judge's nephew. We had talked with him once, and he had even called us in the middle of the night to tell us about two children who needed placement. However, he could offer no legal protection if the mother changed her mind. Now it seemed every other option was a dead end too.

I was still angry, sad, and confused when Paul arrived from his meeting. Over bowls of hot soup, I told him that Peg had called to say there was little hope of adopting a baby now. As I shared the details of the call, I imagined the little red-haired boy she described. We had an extra bedroom in our small house. He might enjoy our ill-behaved puppy. Perhaps we should bring the sled from Paul's mother's attic when we went at Christmas. By the end of the evening I was less sure that the answer would be no.

We had come to this community 16 months before as part of a group ministry project in two adjacent towns sponsored by the National Missions Board of the Presbyterian Church. Paul and Bob were the two ministers employed by the project. In addition, there was an intern from the seminary we had all attended, and the ministers' wives, myself and Jean. The purpose of our work was to try to meet the social needs of the people as well as the spiritual ones. One town was primarily a railroad town; the other, a mining town. Because there was an economic recession, many of the railroad workers and coal miners were unemployed. The women, who worked in small shirt and pocketbook factories for minimum wage, were the sole support of their families.

Paul and Bob were trying to encourage the state to improve the community's inadequate social services. We were involved with many issues: United Mine Workers Hospitals, jobs, nutrition, and bringing new industry to the area. My primary responsibility was programs for children and teens. Because of these programs we had developed close relationships with many of the children in town, and we loved being around them.

Paul and I were living in a newly remodeled house on the only street that went through the lower part of town. Our street was between two small mountains, so the only sun in our yard came for about an hour at high noon. The upper part of town was reached by a street that went straight up the mountain. On the other side of the river was the east side of town, which spread for about 10 blocks above the river bank. Anthracite coal had first been discovered just a few miles from here, and had been mined and sent by a narrow gauge gravity railroad to barges on the river. The metal from the tracks had been sold for scrap in World War II, but the switchback path remained, and we spent many hours walking the dog and hiking on it. I imagined a little boy walking with us.

When Peg called back a week later, I told her we were still thinking about the temporary placement. She said the psychiatrist thought the boy would be ready about the third week in January. "I'll let you know what we decide," I said. "But one more question. Would this affect our chances of getting a baby?" She assured us it would not.

Christmas was a busy time. In the parish, the Christmas parties were important to people who had so little financially. The women's circle had their dinner at a restaurant. For most of these people it was a once-a-year night out. Our group ministry staff enjoyed lots of meals and silly fun times together. Having Bob and Jean's children around was both joyous and frustrating. They were two of the dearest people I knew, but they reminded me of our involuntary childless state. Whenever we stayed overnight with the children so Bob and Jean could get a much needed break, we loved it—but then we had to return to our empty house.

Paul and I spent our Christmas gift money for new ice skates and enjoyed lovely peaceful times on the solidly frozen lake of the nearby state park. When we went to Paul's family on Christmas day, we brought back the sled and a desk and a dollhouse. During the busy days of the holiday season we constantly talked about the pros and cons of having a child for a short time. On the one hand, this placement did not require a long-term commitment; it would certainly be a challenge; and we would experience something of being a family. It might be fun and could help a child. On the other hand, if we enjoyed it, it would be upsetting and disruptive to have it end; it could be too difficult and might be unsuccessful. Finally we realized that we had made up our minds. The ambivalent feelings always ended on the positive side.

We called Peg and said OK. We dug out an old college dorm bedspread, found a small braided rug, brought in a bookcase and filled it with books and magazines we thought a seven-year-old boy would like. And then we waited. As the time approached the ambivalence did not decrease. Then one morning Peg called and told me that the little boy was not making the progress they had hoped and would not be ready for a home placement for a long time. Before the implication of this change of plans had sunk in, she said, "I'd like to come talk to you about another child. We think you'd be perfect for her. She's an older child too, but I want you to hear her story before you say no. Can I see you today?" I invited her for lunch.

In the course of our conversations with Peg about the children with whom we worked, we had come to respect her as a caring and efficient professional, and we enjoyed the warmth of her company. When she arrived for lunch that day, we caught up on the latest news before she told us about the child she wanted to place with us.

"We've cared for Lee Ann for a long time. She's seven now. Her aunt brought her to us, at the age of two, in an extreme state of grief over the death of her mother. After her mother's death this aunt cared for her for a while. Lee Ann missed her mother so much that she cried much of the time. She regressed in toilet training and refused to sleep alone at night. Her aunt was unable to cope with these expressions of grief and brought her to Neighborhood House. They placed her in a foster home in her father's community, and the family often invited the father to visit. Her father suffers emotional illness due to a brain injury in the war and has not been able to care for her. She did well there until the mother of the family had an emotional breakdown because of some other problems we couldn't have foreseen.

"Lee Ann lived at Neighborhood House for a number of months, and then we placed her in a family with five children. The family became unstable and it was not a good place for her. She came back to us, and just a few months ago we placed her with a third family. Unexpectedly, they had to move two weeks ago. She had not been with them long enough for them to consider taking her along. So she is back with us, and she is not a child who does well in group care.

"Her father seems to be losing interest in the relationship, and has had infrequent contact recently. If Lee Ann makes a good adjustment to a placement, he might agree to adoption.

"She is very special to us. We've known her a long time, and we've seen her make good adjustments despite a very difficult situation. She's lively and interested. She attracts the help and concern of the people around her. She needs to be where she will have a lot of attention and caring as soon as possible. She is resilient, but her ability to survive is wearing thin. She has been in families with other children and done well. We think she could adjust to a baby. Don't decide now. Think about it, please."

Paul and I talked and thought this through for a couple of days and several sleepless nights. And then we asked the group ministry to help us think about it. We took seriously our purpose of being supportive to one another as we lived and worked together. They asked the questions we had been asking each other.

"Do you trust the social workers?" Yes, we did. They were both professional and caring. We felt they would tell us the truth and help us.

"What if you really get attached and lose her?" We didn't know what we would do. We were worried about that.

"Isn't it enough—the work you are doing with children here?" No, we still felt unfulfilled. We wanted to have a family, children of our own.

At the end of the morning the uncertainty was still there. Then Bob said, "One thing I know. If you do decide to take Lee Ann, she will have an interesting life."

None of us asked the question that bothered my father in our phone conversation. "What if you become attached and you can't have a positive relationship and she makes you miserable?" My answer to that was, "I can't imagine that happening." We were young and idealistic and we had chosen to work together, hoping to make a positive difference in the world. Our theological training and our work with the extraordinary director of a summer camp for inner-city children had intensified our beliefs: "You can do anything you want to do if you want it enough. Christianity is relevant in the worst places or not at all. Redemption is here and now and in relationship to people." I could not imagine a situation that could not be changed.

My mother expressed her concern, saying, "I can't stand to see you hurt." I couldn't deny that this was a possibility. The conversation with my parents ended with my father's statement: "I'm sure you will make a good decision."

Despite the concern and support we felt from friends and family, no one but us could make the decision. In the end, after all the weighing and balancing, we decided to take Lee Ann because we were strongly drawn to what we knew about this child. We were comfortable with the children we worked with from similar backgrounds. We felt we could make it work. We called Peg and she set a time, three days later, Thursday, January 23rd, for us to go and meet Lee Ann.

My thoughts raced between uncertainties about what time seven-year-olds go to bed and worries about what to wear to the interview. I wanted Lee Ann's first impression of me to be positive. I decided to do away with my care-less blond ponytail, and carefully washed and rolled my hair. At least I'd look older, perhaps even more mature, I thought. I chose my favorite skirt and jacket and red shoes that had been lucky on many occasions. Surely a little girl would like red shoes.

I found myself going through the daily routines and then suddenly thinking, "Oh my gosh, what are we get-ting into?" and just as suddenly feeling very excited—this very weekend she might be here! I told several of the neigh-bors who had elementary school girls about our plans. For the most part, I was a total loss to any of our group minis-try work.

It was a long, slow, snowy drive to Neighborhood House. We were silent, each lost in our own thoughts. I was thinking that as much as we knew about Lee Ann's emotional history and present circumstances, we had no idea of what she looked like or what she liked to do.

Almost as soon as we sat down in Peg's office the door opened a crack. A small thin girl with a mass of brown hair and very large brown eyes peeked around the door. She was wearing a short red, yellow, and green plaid skirt, a somewhat rumpled white blouse, and grubby knee socks that kept falling down. She giggled and ran across the room to hide behind the large desk. Peg told her who we were. From the protected spot behind the desk she jumped up to ask questions. "Do you have a TV?" "Yes, we do." "I don't think I would want to go if you didn't." "Do you have some children?" "No, we don't, but there are lots of children in our neighborhood." She was silent for a while and finally just said "Oh."

Paul said, "We have a dog." She replied uncertainly, "I don't know if I like dogs." "Our dog is a puppy and he's friendly," Paul answered. I said, "We have a dollhouse you can play with." "Can I use real water?" she asked. "Sure," I answered. "It will be your dollhouse." "OK. I would like that," she replied.

The only visible sign that this was not just an ordinary visit between adults and a child was a raw chapped ring around Lee Ann's mouth. Her tongue shot out, making it redder and more angry.

Peg had left us alone to visit with Lee Ann. When she returned Lee Ann said, "Well, good-bye now. I'm going to eat skaghetti at a church," and she was gone.

Peg thought the interview had gone well. I had to admit that, in this brief encounter, I liked Lee Ann. She had interviewed us as much as we interviewed her. She was genuinely excited about new things—the "skaghetti" supper she was going to in a few minutes as well as coming to our house. She liked Peg, and that affection was mutual and real. We talked about arrangements and medical history, and agreed to keep careful records of what the monthly payments covered and what we spent ourselves, to help them see if the payments were adequate. We agreed to pick her up at Neighborhood House Friday after school.

The trip home was relaxed and a bit giddy. Lee Ann was all we expected and more. Just as Peg had said, she attracted interest and concern. We wanted to help this charming child feel secure. It was clear that whatever we did together, Lee Ann would have her input. We liked that. We felt ever more confident that our decision was the right one. We talked nonstop about the practical details: who in the neighborhood to invite to play, what to tell people in the church about her, what to cook for our first meal together. We also talked about larger issues. What kind of emotional supports would she need? What kind would we need? If it did work out, and, as Peg had said, she became available for adoption, how wonderful that would be!

When we arrived at Neighborhood House on Friday, Lee Ann was running around collecting her belongings and saying good-bye to friends. We went with Peg to look at the clothes room, where we could come and get things if we needed them. She said, "We like for the children to be as well dressed as and have the same opportunity as others in the community. When I come down in a week, maybe we can talk about lessons or clubs that would help Lee Ann."

When we came back Lee Ann and a cute little red-haired girl were excitedly going through a small cardboard box, which I later learned contained everything Lee Ann possessed except for a doll carriage and a doll from Christmas. "Oh, boy, jeans. Three pairs. All new! And look at this great shirt!" Peg helped us carry the bag and the box to the car. Lee Ann became very quiet and held the doll tightly. We said good-bye to Peg and the red-haired girl.

On the trip home we tried to have a conversation, but Lee Ann answered every question with one polite word. We tried to sing, but we had no repertoire of songs in common. Finally, in desperation, I suggested that we get off at the next exit and get an ice cream cone. That brought a silent smile.

Back in the car, things were a little more relaxed, and I said, "Next Friday is your birthday. Do you have any ideas—something you would like to do?" "Sure," she said, "a party." Surprised, I answered, "But you don't know any children yet." "By next Friday I will. Children who have families have parties." And that was that.

When we arrived home, while Lee Ann was looking at the dollhouse and putting her things away, I fixed what I thought was every child's dream meal—hamburgers, carrot sticks, and potato chips. But when we sat down to eat, she took only a couple of small bites. I asked, "Don't you like hamburgers?" "No," she whispered. Not wanting her to go to bed hungry on her very first night, I asked her what she did like to eat. "Tuna fish and chicken noodle soup," she said. I found a can of tuna, mixed it up, and spread it on a bun. She smiled at the familiar food and began to eat. Little did I know then that tuna fish and chicken noodle soup were almost the only foods she liked.

By the time supper was over it was dark and getting late. We sat down in the living room and she said, "The dog is OK." I suggested she might want to take a bath before bed, and I ran bathwater. She went into the bathroom and closed the door, and later came out wearing her pj's. "Well, good night," she said. I asked her if she would like a story. "OK," she replied. And she listened politely to a story that Paul read. We turned out the light and in a few minutes she appeared to be asleep. She is too good to be true, I thought. She seemed to go right to sleep, but I tossed and turned and thought about the future, which loomed with great uncertainty.

For the next several days, Lee Ann was willing to play any game we suggested and to converse on any topic— with one-word replies. She was a helper in the kitchen, a cleaner of the yard, and she kept her room neat as could be. She went dutifully, if unenthusiastically, to school, and after several days waited on the corner for the town bus to take her to school with children from the neighborhood.

The one exception to this perfect behavior was with other children. We invited a neighborhood child to play. I heard a loud commotion and found Lee Ann in one corner of the room. She was tightly clutching a whole armful of games and toys, and the neighbor was disappearing through the front door. "What's the matter?" I said. "She wanted to play with these things. I live here. They're not hers. She was mean to me." That particular child didn't come back for a long time.

True to her word, she knew children at school by Friday. We invited them and the children from our neighborhood to a party, complete with cake, balloons, and party hats. She was all smiles when the children handed her the brightly wrapped gifts. But later in the party, when someone else wanted a turn with a toy, her face looked like a storm cloud. After everyone had left, she surveyed the newly acquired toys and said with a deep, relaxed sigh, "I had a real party." In contrast to her apparent feeling of success, I was exhausted and felt we had barely survived.

When Peg came to see us, Paul and I talked with her before Lee Ann came home from school. We told her about the super-good behavior and how difficult we were finding it to make real contact. I thought that this covered over some intense feelings she didn't feel safe enough to talk about or show through her behavior. We told Peg that we didn't know whether she was really happy and comfortable with us.

Lee Ann was extremely glad to see Peg, and more relaxed than she had been since she arrived. Peg took Lee Ann out to the ice cream store where they could talk privately. When they returned, Peg accepted our invitation to stay for supper and came into the kitchen to help, where she told me, "Lee Ann thinks things here are nearly perfect. She really wants to stay, and she thought the party was wonderful!"

We had a pleasant meal, with Lee Ann getting information about her friends at Neighborhood House and sending messages. As she left, Peg gave Lee Ann a birthday package from her father. She excitedly tore into it and pulled out a very fancy party dress. We said good-bye to Peg. Then we talked about how much fun we had, and Lee Ann was humming a happy song as she got ready for bed. I took the dress into the bedroom to hang it up. I looked at the label. The black velveteen top said, "Dry Clean Only." The pink flocked skirt said, "Do Not Dry Clean." They were sewed together. "Oh, boy," I thought. "We'll hope it never gets dirty."

Lee Ann began to enjoy being outside with the neighborhood children. Outdoors, she seemed more willing to share. We made snow people, and on days when the sun shone, there were games, tree climbing, and hours spent carefully crossing the creek, trying not to fall in.

When Lee Ann had been with us three weeks, I realized I was frustrated about still not being able to make good contact. I'd never had this experience with a child before. I missed the easy rapport that I'd had with the children from the church. I was home more after school, not working as much with their programs, and they didn't quite know how Lee Ann fit into their relationship with me. I also missed the close kind of sharing Paul and I had done when we came in from work—about the people we worked with, ideas, and just things in general.

It was hard to talk about the past. Lee Ann didn't know the people, even our families. It was hard to talk about the future. None of us knew what the summer would bring, much less next year. There was only so much in the present, and with Lee Ann carefully watching everything we said and did, even that was difficult. Her large brown eyes never missed a detail. Her tongue moved constantly around her mouth, making it raw, and letting us know that she was not as calm as she appeared.

There were, however, getting to be moments when things seemed to work. We went to New York for the circus, ate dinner at the automat, and bought Lee Ann ice skates at Macy's. On the way home, the lights of the city had come on. She was relaxed and happy, and exclaimed, "Oh, city, you interest me." We went skating at the state park. She held on to our hands and finally moved five feet alone across the ice. She was so pleased with herself that she was still giggling and talking about it when, tired and cold, we reached the state park lodge for hot chocolate.

There were many good times with the group ministry staff. Bob and Jean's children, because they were younger, were no threat, and she was motherly and very imaginative with them. In late February we had a day of surprisingly warm and sunny weather. Lee Ann was tired and muddy after playing out all day. When she went in to take her bath she invited me to come in and visit, and with unconcealed joy she said, "The feelings inside me thought it was spring all day."

In mid-March, Paul's sister Connie was married in our small sanctuary. We all had fun helping her with her plans. Connie was very generous in sharing her special day with Lee Ann and a same-age cousin. She helped both girls to feel special.

There were also beginning to be brief times when Lee Ann showed annoyance. "These socks are all wrong. They're not white enough. They're stretched out." "Just look at the rickrack on this dress—it's all wrinkled." "I can't find my doll's best dress." But very quickly she would become her controlled self again.

She was extremely curious, always asking questions. She wanted to know how things worked, what we meant when we used words she didn't know. We became aware there were great gaps in her ordinary knowledge. She didn't know the difference between a penny, a nickel, and a dime. She went to the store for me, which was a block away, to pick up an item for dinner. We had quite a conversation about how much money to pay and how to make change. She had no concept of time, and we began by counting time as one or two or three cartoons on the TV. Everything about the human body interested her, and none of the information we gave her was familiar. She asked question after question.

At about the same time her teacher and I came to the conclusion that she was really good at faking it, but she was not reading at all. It was the same with numbers. We put a bowl of fruit on the table and began counting apples and oranges. But this didn't seem to help. "There's just too much else to deal with," I thought.

We spent lots of time making things: cookies, doll clothes, a house from a cardboard box for her toy cat. Her room was beginning to look like an ordinary kid room, with posters and pictures on the wall and a respectable collection of toys and books about.

It was now April, almost three months since she had come. It seemed like a long time to us and we were very attached to her. More and more we felt like a family. She still tried to avoid any form of address to us, mostly referring to us as "you," and except for very brief exceptions, she was still very well behaved and careful. Something happened that reminded me why this was so. Our friend Jean knew that she was trying to learn to tell time, so she gave her a beautiful pink alarm clock. Lee Ann said, "Thank you. It's very pretty." And then she asked, "Can I take it with me when I go?"

Peg called to tell us she would like to visit on Thursday and that Lee Ann's father had called requesting a visit. We told Lee Ann about these approaching events. She was excited about Peg coming, but it was impossible to read her reaction about her father. She made her usual statement when we asked anything about him. "I will probably go take care of his house when I'm a teenager, but that's a long time, you know."

When Peg came we talked about the school problems. We found out that because of the conditions of the family where she lived at the time, the school system had allowed Lee Ann to start first grade, which was all day, at age five and a half. This explained why she was so young for her third grade placement. Peg said the staff at Neighborhood House had not noticed any particular difficulty, but they probably didn't keep up with such things very closely. When we told her how calm Lee Ann was, Peg suggested that it might not always be like this—that in the near future we might look back upon these days of relative calm with nostalgia.

On the day of the trip to Neighborhood House to visit her father, Lee Ann had a short fuse. Breakfast wasn't right. The dress she chose to wear had wrinkles. There were knots in her hair and it hurt when I combed it. She couldn't find her favorite stuffed animal to take in the car. And the circle around her mouth, which had improved somewhat, was very raw again. One by one we solved these problems. Grape juice replaced orange juice. The skirt got a quick press. We found the stuffed animal under the bed. We put some lotion on her face.

When we arrived at Neighborhood House, Mr. Steinkohler was waiting in the parlor. We could tell immediately that he was Lee Ann's father. He was a small, lean man with expressive brown eyes just like hers. In a good mood, he was charming and smiling. I thought they would like to visit alone and started to get up. Lee Ann said, "Please stay." She was very quiet. He talked to her in a teasing sort of way. "Well, I guess you're probably making these people crazy." She answered his questions that required answers with short sentences. Finally she asked, "How is granddaddy?" "He's OK, I guess."

In about 10 minutes Lee Ann looked from us to her father, not seeming to know who to ask. Then, to no one in particular, she said, "I'm going to find Jenny," and was off up the steps to the children's living quarters.

Mr. Steinkohler began to tell us about his work, addressing all his remarks to Paul. He was soon telling the kinds of stories about coal mining our parishioners told, about his fear of cave-ins. He was the person who lighted the dynamite, and he said he was always afraid. Paul answered in his pastoral tone, and soon Mr. Steinkohler was deep in conversation about his problems with Paul.

I left them alone and found Peg in her office. She took me up to meet Momma Miller, who was Lee Ann's favorite staff person, and as I talked with her she told me how much she missed Lee Ann.

When we came back, Mr. Steinkohler was standing at the door and Paul was using the phone. Peg explained that Mr. Steinkohler had lost the ability to read in the accident during the war in which he had suffered brain damage. Paul was calling a taxi. We stood at the door and visited until the taxi came. He made no further effort to see Lee Ann or tell her good-bye. His final words to me were, "Let me know if she misbehaves. I'll loan you the cat-of-nine-tails we have in the mines." He laughed, and I replied, "I don't think that will be necessary."

After he left, Peg remarked that we had probably seen him at his best. When we went to tell Lee Ann we needed to go, she didn't seem surprised or upset that her father had left. Jenny and another friend walked to the door with us. As they watched us walk to the car, Lee Ann slipped one hand into each of ours and smiled to her friends.

On the way home she said, "Let's sing." We tried many verses of "Old MacDonald" and then she sang her made-up songs and we tried to follow. We stopped for ice cream and then we sang some more.

Things had gone smoothly now for a long time, with the short flashes of temper that occurred every few days brought quickly under control. At night when she was asleep I thought about the day—how "good" she was, how I was almost too calm, too patient, and how tired I was at the end of each day from being constantly on guard. I felt there were lots of unknown and unexpressed emotions beneath the surface in all of us. I didn't know what would happen if I told her I was tired of chicken noodle soup and we needed to eat something else now, or if I couldn't keep up the laundry and kitchen cleaning chores to make the house appear near perfect. If she knew I sometimes got angry, would she want to leave, or be hurt forever? What if I couldn't be a perfect parent, or even an adequate one?

On a cold, rainy Saturday late in April the emotional dam broke. We had planned a picnic that had to be moved indoors. Paul got several emergency calls from parishioners that took him away. He also needed to work on his sermon for Sunday. I took Lee Ann with me to the grocery store, and then she played pretty much alone with her dolls and the dollhouse. We had a simple, early supper and I was working on the dishes when she came in and asked to go to the store. I told her that all the stores were closed and asked what she needed. "My doll's feet are cold. Her shoes aren't warm enough."

I suggested that when I finished the dishes, we could make some boots from a piece of felt. "The things you make are no good," she shouted. "She needs real shoes." By this time Lee Ann's tears were dripping down her face.

"I'm sorry. No stores are open now." I said that I, too, was feeling very upset because she was so frustrated. "This is just the way it always is," she yelled. "Nothing good ever happens to me."

She ran from the room. I heard what sounded like books hitting the floor, toys falling down. When I reached the door, the bookcase was turned over and Lee Ann was throwing a shoe at the wall, screaming again and again, "Nothing good ever happens to me, nothing good ever happens."

I walked over to put my arms around her, but she pulled away and threw herself on the floor, kicking and screaming. About this time Paul heard the noise and arrived to see what was the matter. He tried to talk to Lee Ann. The screaming got louder. I tried to touch her. The kicking became more violent. Finally, not knowing what in the world to do, I sat down on the bed, and Paul did too. She kicked and screamed for a very long time, interrupting to say over and over, "Nothing good ever happens." When she became quieter she said, "Even the doll I got for Christmas got its arm torn off while I went out to eat. Nothing good ever happens."

I sat down on the floor next to Lee Ann and she told me the whole story of a tiny doll from her Christmas stocking she had left in her cubby while she went to eat Christmas dinner. When she came back, some other children had pulled the arms and legs off, and it couldn't be fixed. I didn't know what to say or do. Finally I said, "I'm sorry." I picked her up and sat in the rocking chair with her on my lap and rocked and rocked and rocked. Paul sat on the bed looking miserable. Finally Lee Ann relaxed and was asleep. Paul carried her to her bed and covered her up. I was completely exhausted, and Paul and I were too devastated to talk about what had happened. We went to bed and finally, completely spent, I fell asleep.

The next morning when I got up, Paul was unhappily struggling with his sermon and Lee Ann was still quietly in her room with the door closed. I knocked on the door uneasily and she said, almost in a whisper, "Come in." I had picked up the bookcase and some of the books the night before, but I didn't want to wake her, so the floor was still cluttered with game pieces and toys. She was picking them up. "Let me help you," I said. She was silent, but her eyes told me what she was thinking. "Oh, boy, I've done it now. I guess I'll have to leave." I wanted to reassure her.

"I'm sorry you were so unhappy last night," I said, "but it's OK. Families tell their feelings to each other." We continued to pick up the toys in silence. And then I said, "Come on, let's fix breakfast and get ready for Sunday School."

Over many weeks these periods of complete loss of control alternated with the attempt to be super-good. It was probably a week and a half before it happened again. And then the temper tantrums became more and more frequent. It began to feel like we were on the down section of a roller coaster. At the end of each of these episodes Lee Ann told us more and more about her life experiences. How she had asked for an extra helping of food in one foster home and had been hit by the father. How she always felt less important and less cared about than the "real" children in these other families. How she loved Momma Miller and liked it when she was a little bit sick and could stay home all alone with her.

We quickly learned some things about handling these tempers. It did no good to try to talk with Lee Ann or make contact of any kind while she was so upset. We stayed nearby, but not within sight. When she became calmer we talked it out. These angry times were triggered by small frustrations in our daily life. For example, the dress she wanted to wear was dirty. Or she did not want to go to school because something about her situation was not perfect. Sometimes there was just a buildup of little things that weren't pleasing. The common factors were that someone else was wrong and everything had always been wrong for her.

One day it was just too much for me, and I yelled back at her, "It really isn't my fault that your life has been so bad." I felt terrible. This child had legitimate complaints, and I, the adult, could not even be patient enough to let her express them in the only way she could at that moment. I talked to Peg about this and she said it was natural for me to feel angry with her blaming me, and it was probably good for both of us for me to express it.

Another time, after she had become calm enough to talk, I said, "Lee Ann, repeat after me: 'I, Lee Ann Steinkohler, can sometimes make a mistake.'" I talked to her about how sometimes she was responsible for things happening, and how I wished we could talk about it before it got so big and she needed to blame someone else. I told her I always loved her but I was angry with her sometimes.

Even during the worst of these times, Paul and I talked to each other. We felt that the struggles were depressing and demoralizing, but our family was worth the effort. We believed in the power of love and the possibility of change. Except for Peg, there was no professional help close to us, and we had to work out the problems one day at a time. If we tried something and it didn't work, we renegotiated. When it did work, we remembered it so we could repeat our successes.

Jean was my sane voice on the other end of the telephone. When I talked to her about these devastating episodes, she said, "Maybe when you begin to see more good days than bad ones, that will be progress." Very gradually, this began to happen. In spite of the emotional downs, Lee Ann's play relationships were better. She was enjoying tremendously learning to swim at the "Y." She was beginning to be able to separate joking comments from the truth. "I know that what you just said is a joke." And she would smile. We were having days and days when it was fun to have her around, absorbing new information and sharing her imaginative world with us.

One day, when I had explained why she couldn't visit a friend from school overnight, she said, "Is what you told me the real truth?" I realized it was a half truth, and that for Lee Ann, this would not do. So I said, "No, there's more. I don't know if her mother will stay home all night. That might be scary for you. You can't go, but we'll make plans to invite her to come here."

In the meantime, the end of the school year was rapidly approaching. It was unclear whether Neighborhood House needed to ask Mr. Steinkohler about taking Lee Ann on our summer trips. The relationship between Lee Ann and Mr. Steinkohler on the one hand and Neighborhood

House on the other was voluntary, and the custody issue had never been decided by the court. We had no real doubts about his permission, but it took a long time for him to respond. This was a reminder that, although we made the everyday decisions, as foster parents we had no control over many areas of Lee Ann's life.

At the beginning of the summer we took a sleeper from Philadelphia and woke up at midnight to watch them change our car to a train going toward my parents' home. Lee Ann, at the age of eight, had never ridden on a train. My parents had made a short trip to visit us during the spring, but this was Lee Ann's first visit to their house. My mother and father and my 19-year-old sister Ann, who was home from college, met us at the train. Lee Ann was excited about this larger family, and when she met great-grandparents and great-aunts and uncles, she was truly ecstatic. Mother had lunch ready for us, and in her excitement, Lee Ann put sugar in the chicken noodle soup instead of the iced tea. She thought this was very funny.

Later, every time she thought about it, she would giggle and say, "Remember when we were at Nanna's and I put sugar in the chicken noodle soup?" This spontaneous experience, the kind that makes up so much of the fabric of a shared family life, had been mostly lacking for us, and we enjoyed it.

Lee Ann's behavior was not always within the accepted norms. But her language and cultural patterns were like those of the other children we knew in our community. It was a surprise to me, as we visited childhood friends and their children, how different from them Lee Ann was. She appeared young and very unsophisticated compared to our friends' children of the same age. She was certainly streetwise, but she didn't know the more subtle ways of interacting with others. Her pronunciation and grammar were different.

She remained under a kind of relaxed emotional control most of the time, but there were several brief outbursts of temper while we were at my parents' house. My father said, "A self-respecting sailor would be glad to have a vocabulary like hers." My mother restated her fear of my getting hurt. Throughout the visit, they were both warm and accepting of Lee Ann, and she enjoyed them very much. My sister Ann was an exciting, active college student, who was performing as a dancer in an outdoor drama. She knew all about clothes and music. Her friends constantly dropped in. Lee Ann enjoyed doing things with Ann and just being with her.

This visit stirred up many feelings in me. I felt protective of Lee Ann and defensive about her, overexplaining her behavior. I was upset with myself for feeling embarrassed about her cultural differences. Friends asked, "Do you think you'll ever be able to really love her?" and my answer that I loved her now seemed not to convince them. Paul and I had chosen work and a lifestyle different from these friends' choices. But up until this time, I had assumed that at any moment, if I wanted to, I could step back into this life again, and that when we visited, I could be like them and still be myself. It began to seem that Lee Ann's arrival had affected this choice.

If I believed, as I did, that she should be judged acceptable and successful on the basis of positive movement from where she had started, rather than on some arbitrary standard, I was moving away from the traditional standards of my friends. Perhaps I couldn't really have it both ways.

When we arrived back home, things were in full swing for the second year of children's summer day camp. The camp was free for ages six through 16. The parents' only obligation was to attend a Wednesday night family picnic with parent education programs and family fun activities. We held the camp in the woods surrounding a small Episcopal mission church, using the building for office space and rainy day activities. The previous year Paul had been the director, Bob and our seminary intern and I were counselors, and the Episcopal priest was general troubleshooter.

The camp was very popular, so this year we had asked for help. We were listed in "Invest Your Summer," a brochure sent to college students all over the country. From their applications we had chosen six, who would arrive in less than a week. I was paid a small salary to work with the students and help with the planning. I used this to hire a person to clean and iron and do some baby-sitting a few hours a week. The female students would live in a couple of rooms next door to us. The boys were to stay with Margaret, a parishioner who lived on top of the hill, who would feed the whole group. We chose Margaret, a sixtyish woman who cleaned the power company offices after hours, because we thought she would be an interesting and caring person for the students to get to know.

When Lee Ann first came to us, Margaret told us that she went to work on the same bus the children rode down the hill from school. She had apparently told the other children, "You mess with her and you mess with me." Lee Ann need have no fears with such a protector.

I was looking forward to camp beginning. I had felt it was necessary to be completely focused on Lee Ann for these first months. Now I needed to be involved in other things too. Lee Ann would be in the middle group. One of the students would be her counselor.

We hoped the assistance of the college students would free Paul and Bob to do other things, and in many ways it did. The students were lively and talented people who brought stimulation and excitement not only to the camp, but to the whole community. Although they were inexperienced in working with children, they cared deeply about them and formed close relationships. They took their jobs seriously and spent hours at our house talking about the problems of individual children and of the groups, and sharing their own feelings. Because most of these students came from affluent families, they were profoundly shocked at the extent of the poverty in our community. They loved Margaret, and she was their honest but jovial guide to the local culture.

For Lee Ann, having her parents involved in a program like this, particularly one that involved her, was a new experience. It made her feel special, and I sometimes heard her say to another child, "You better not do that. My parents are the boss of this camp." The group experience in a nonacademic setting with a good counselor was also a tremendous boost to her self-confidence. She was able to be a leader here, even if it sometimes meant leading children to fall in the creek. Having the counselors around our house meant that much more attention for her, that many more people to confront with her honest questions. "Do you have a boyfriend?" "What's it like to have a boyfriend?" "What do you mean you go to school away from where your parents live?" They were introducing her to a wider world. The students, unanimously, were taken with her charm and startled by her language and her outbursts of angry feelings.

At times, Lee Ann was reluctant to share my time and attention with the students. When I was working with them, she would parade through the room time and again with requests for attention. We had to discuss this issue many times. The students' comments and their concern for Lee Ann were mostly helpful. I had told them her mother died when she was two, that she had lived in three different foster homes in addition to a children's home, and that she struggled academically and socially at school. They observed her in the camp group doing things that annoyed other children, such as always wanting to be first and to get the counselor's attention all for herself. The students talked to me about their own feelings of abandonment in their childhoods and what they wished had happened to them.

For me it was a good, if busy, summer. I was glad to see Lee Ann happy and growing. I enjoyed the students. Their questions about programs and methods of working with children helped me to think through my philosophy clearly and to express it so they could understand—why we needed to work individually, how we encouraged the children to take responsibility, what was the best way to approach parents. I found myself very defensive about our people. As the students got to know them better, they understood why a mother who had so little might choose to buy a few minutes' happiness with soft drinks for her children rather than a quart of milk. I was also pleased that, through the day camp, I was able to re-establish a relationship with the older children who had felt displaced by Lee Ann.

At first, Lee Ann was put off by having other kids hanging around "her" house to see me, but later on she was able to accept them. Another tremendous bonus for Lee Ann was the outdoor experience. She loved every creature, from deer to salamanders. Paul and I liked camping, and on several weekends we took our tent to the state park. Lee Ann enjoyed every bit of it, from washing the dishes outdoors to telling stories around the campfire and all of us going to sleep at the same time in the tent. She even added several new foods to her growing list of favorites.

Earlier in the summer Peg had offered us a chance to get away without Lee Ann for a weekend or so. We were indignant. It would certainly be more fun with her. When summer camp ended, we packed our camping equipment and our dog and spent several weeks on an island off the coast of North Carolina.

Lee Ann saw the ocean for the first time, but without a bit of fear. She was in the waves from the first moment to the last. She was an avid collector of sea shells, examining each one carefully and asking, "Who do you think lived here?" She was not bothered by blowing sand, mosquitoes, or rain. It seemed to us that the six months she had been with us was a long time. We had experienced a lot together, and we were really a family now. So after an argument about whether she would get out of the cold water, I was surprised when she screamed, "You don't care a bit about me!"

"Don't you trust me at all?" I asked. Tears rolled down her face and she said, "I don't know. I just don't know." I couldn't believe that six months had made so little difference, and I wondered if Lee Ann would ever be able to trust us.

After the camping trip we headed home. Another visit with Mr. Steinkohler reminded us again of the source of the uncertain feelings Lee Ann had expressed at the beach. Mr. Steinkohler said he was pleased to have Lee Ann stay with us. Once again, he visited only briefly with her, talked with Paul, and left. Once again, Lee Ann was upset before the visit and relieved afterwards.

After our successful summer as a family, Paul and I were feeling optimistic about the fall. We had worked with phonics workbooks and counted objects all summer. Lee

Ann had enjoyed trying to read road signs and advertising billboards. We were hopeful that this would translate into academic progress, but when school began we immediately realized it didn't. Her curiosity, evident everywhere else, was absent at school.

She liked her teacher, but the work was overwhelming. There were more and more mornings when she said she was sick, only to feel much better by 11 o'clock. When Peg came we worked out a plan to send Lee Ann to school every day unless she had a temperature or some very overt symptom. This caused a lot of early morning unhappiness. Occasionally I had to wait until she was calm and take her late. She didn't like going late, and gradually accepted that school was a regular obligation.

She was often angry about having to wear her old heavy school jacket rather than a pretty lightweight pink jacket we had bought last spring. Finally, I made a chart of temperatures, put it next to an outdoor thermometer, and we let the thermometer decide. She was learning to ride my old bicycle, continued swimming at the "Y," and went to an afterschool program that our group ministry sponsored.

She and a friend down the street built a fort. She received invitations to birthday parties and spend-the-nights. She seemed ambivalent about our limits. Occasionally, she went home with children after school without permission. One day I located her and said, "Start walking. You didn't tell me you were going home with the twins." She replied, "OK, Mrs. Crabapple, I'm walking." But she didn't protest very much. I concluded she was testing where the limits were and also how much we cared about her.

While she was at school I continued some group ministry work. Our staff meetings gave me an opportunity for stimulating adult conversation, and I enjoyed my contact with people in the parishes. While Lee Ann was at the afterschool program, I made an extensive wardrobe for a doll we had bought for Christmas. We had visits from our parents and went to Paul's family for Thanksgiving, where Lee Ann had fun with the cousin she had met at Aunt Connie's wedding.

We began our preparations for Christmas as soon as Advent began. We were supporting a child from Korea, and we sent him a Christmas box. Lee Ann carefully picked out the strongest truck and the warmest sweater to send. She told us how she had felt about receiving things from strangers. "They shouldn't break," she said. We baked cookies by the hundreds and boxed them and took them to shut-ins on snowy evenings. We made cards and gifts for her to take to her father and grandfather.

On a Sunday, which turned out to be the day of the evening Christmas program at our church, we went to see Lee Ann's father at Neighborhood House. Lee Ann had been very uneasy about this visit. At the final rehearsal of the verses each child was to say individually, she couldn't remember a word. She became sullen and refused to try. Her Sunday School teacher and the director of the Christmas program alternately tried to threaten and cajole her. The director said, "If you don't say your piece, you can't have ice cream." The teacher said, "Of course she can, I'll bring it to her here." Finally, I interceded and said, "She's pretty upset right now. It's OK if she doesn't say the piece, but she can't have ice cream on the carpet. Come sit with the other children, Lee Ann."

This situation was typical of the advice outsiders offered, which fell into two extreme types: either to expect nothing of Lee Ann because of her special problems or to discipline her severely. Our course was somewhere in between. We expected a lot of her, but when she didn't meet expectations we renegotiated and tried again.

After the visit with her father early Sunday afternoon, when we were coming home in the car, Lee Ann kept saying her Christmas piece over and over, and she told us she wanted to be in the program. She performed faultlessly.

And what to say about Christmas itself? When our photos were developed, the one of Christmas morning said it all—a little girl in a Christmas nightgown holding a doll in a matching nightgown under a Christmas tree. Her smile could have lighted an entire city.

Christmas Eve started with a group ministry staff dinner at our house. Lee Ann and Jean's son John played Mary and Joseph under the Christmas tree. The warmth of the season and close friends made all of us feel good. At 11 o'clock we had a Christmas Eve service in the church in the other part of our parish, where Bob and Jean lived. The people in this town were wonderfully warmhearted. The candles and the traditional carols and readings were joyful, and we went happily home through the crisp night.

There were other gifts—a clay pinch pot Lee Ann made at school for me; a bookmark for Paul; books, records, and games for Lee Ann. But none of that really mattered. The important thing was that we belonged together. We were a family.

Part 2

On January 24th, 1959, we had a group ministry supper at our house, complete with a cake, to celebrate Lee Ann's having been with us a year. For Paul and me it was a happy occasion, symbolizing the feeling of family and how much Lee Ann meant to us. For Lee Ann, the whole day was a disaster, and as I tried to figure out why, it became clear that this landmark symbolized something else for her— an adjustment that might not be permanent. She still was afraid of being removed at any moment.

The relationship with her father was hard for her to understand. "Why don't I see him more often?" "You see him when he asks." "Why doesn't he ask more often?" "I don't know." Focusing on his long absences made her feel very insecure. I realized, once again, how much hurt remained from her early losses, and how long it would take to heal those hurts.

The New Year had begun with more than the usual degree of uncertainty in our lives. We had done an annual report of how we had spent the money we were receiving from Presbyterian National Missions. That money and an endowment fund of the congregation supported our three-year experimental project, which was now finished. We felt good about our work. We hoped National Missions would pick up the amount no longer paid by the endowment and add to the total. Salaries at their present level simply could not pay family expenses, and our project could not continue without an increased contribution. We hoped that the money would be approved, but we felt uneasy as we waited for the answer.

In addition, Peg had called us earlier in the month to tell us that she thought they would have a baby for us in the early spring. We knew that the mother had three months after the baby was born to change her mind and that Neighborhood House didn't place babies before that time. Peg gave us this information early, at the risk of disappointing us later, to give us more time to prepare Lee Ann. We could move her to the larger attic bedroom now so she wouldn't be displaced by the baby. We had time, too, to help her work toward greater independence. We were very excited, of course, but we couldn't buy anything or prepare for this event because we were afraid it wouldn't work out. It was a wonderful but very strange time.

When I asked Lee Ann if she would like to have the big room upstairs as her bedroom, she was delighted. Her birthday was the 31st of January. We decided to have her party in the attic room, then she could move in the next week. She was very excited about her birthday, so we began to put posters and pictures on the walls to decorate them, both for the party and for when it was her bedroom. The children she invited were friends who had been to our house to play. As she planned the party, Lee Ann had talked about what individual children liked. We chose games that were fun and didn't focus on winning.

Lee Ann was all smiles as she greeted her guests and carefully stacked the gifts to open later on. When she opened the gifts, she left them on the table for everyone to examine and play with. At the end, Lee Ann declared that her party was wonderful, and her guests seemed to agree.

Around the middle of February, Paul and Bob got an answer from National Missions. Although they really liked our project and thought it was important, the National Missions Board had decided to spend most of their money in cities with large populations. The Board suggested that unemployed people from our small towns could move to places where jobs were more plentiful. The missions board would continue to support the two small churches, but not at the level of funding we needed.

We were frustrated. Only a few of the younger members of our churches had skills and flexibility enough to move if they lost their jobs. But even those who did move usually became so homesick they would be back in a few months. For ourselves, the Board's decision meant we could not continue here as a group ministry.

We had many options to explore. We wanted to find a place where the group could go together, but our search hadn't yielded any good possibilities.

We asked Peg what our move would mean for our keeping Lee Ann, as well as for adopting a baby. The baby was not a problem. The agency could work out the adoption wherever we went. The situation with Lee Ann, however, was different. As long as we stayed in the state there was no problem. If we moved to another state, however, we might have to give her up.

Janet, the social worker who had worked with Lee Ann from the time she was two until about two years ago, had returned. She and Peg both talked to us about not making a job decision based solely on Lee Ann. They were afraid we would regret it later. They assured us that children are resilient, that Lee Ann had adjusted before, that she was not our responsibility.

But she was our responsibility. She was finally beginning to trust us. Would she ever try again? We loved Lee Ann. She was family, and we couldn't imagine our lives without her. I was furious. We wanted to adopt Lee Ann and that, of course, would also solve the problem. But we knew it was too soon to discuss this with Mr. Steinkohler. He had been more interested in her since the placement with us than for several years before, and I was sure one year did not seem long to him. The judge in his county turned down cases much clearer than this all the time.

Mr. Steinkohler had visited with her for a total of 30 minutes in the last year, and his sole financial contribution was a birthday present a year ago. But this far exceeded the requirements of the law as it related to adoption.

Although we were powerless in the matter of adoption, we had to keep Lee Ann with us. We decided to stay in the state. Bob and Jean needed more money and could not consider staying. Finally, Bob accepted a job in a neighborhood center in Cleveland, where his family could live within about 15 minutes of his work.

We thought about staying on in our community, but without the support of a team ministry Paul would not be able to do many of the things that made a difference. With two children, I was not going to be as available to help either. I couldn't imagine life here without Jean on the other end of the telephone line, without a team for discussing ideas. We explored other possibilities in the state but found nothing that would give us the chance to continue our work on social issues.

Then one day when Paul came home, he said, "You know, I've been thinking. One of the things I liked best about our work here was the work camps with the college students. Maybe in the campus ministry I could work on social issues 'from the other side.'" It seemed like a good idea.

He went to Philadelphia and talked to the national executive of campus ministry for the Presbyterian Church, but came home feeling frustrated. There were exciting jobs in campus ministry that would enable him to do the things he believed in, but not in our state.

I was full of conflicting feelings: excitement over the baby who might soon be ours; sadness and grief at the end of the church project; uncertainty as to what life in our town would be like without our work; and anger because there were too many important things in my life over which I had no control. We tried not to talk about our problems when Lee Ann was home, but she knew, of course.

In early March, when Bob and Jean accepted their new job and we knew they would leave in June, we told Lee Ann. She was very upset over the impending change. We reassured her that *we* were not moving away from her. And so the question that had never even been a question was settled. We also told her that we thought we were going to have a baby to adopt soon; that she would be the big sister; and that I would need a lot of help, because she probably knew more about babies than I did. She was excited, but apprehensive, and sometimes she had a strange expression on her face.

I wondered if she was feeling she had been through these things before and they hadn't worked out very well. She was quieter than usual.

Finally, as the job search continued to yield nothing where we were, Paul called Peg and asked her where we could legally take Lee Ann. She didn't know, but she told us she would try to work it out in any state that didn't have a law prohibiting bringing in foster children. She gave Paul a number to call in Washington to find out what states those were. In 15 minutes, Paul had a list of possible states. Then he called the campus ministry executive and told him he would like to know about campus ministry jobs in those states, and he began to fill out the forms the executive had given him several weeks before.

Meanwhile, our daily life and the life of the parish went on. Lee Ann had homework and neighborhood play, and we all went ice skating. No matter what happened, we expected to be here in the summer, and we were planning for the summer camps.

Easter was in late March. I had almost finished a new dress I was making for Lee Ann as well as one for myself. On the Monday of Easter week Peg called. "Can you come tomorrow to see the baby?" I was so excited I could hardly answer. Of course we could. "Don't buy anything until you see him," she said. "He is awfully big."

I found Paul and told him the good news. I called Jean, and she offered to lend us what we needed and, when it was time, to advise me what to buy. When Lee Ann came home from school we couldn't resist going out and buying one stuffed toy. She chose a pink rabbit with rubber ears.

Early the next morning Lee Ann arrived in our room. "I don't feel good." She was hot with fever. School was out of the question. I gave her orange juice and something for fever and put her back to bed. "What about the baby?" she said. "We'll see. I'm going to call the doctor when it's late enough." It wasn't even light. I felt torn. I would never leave Lee Ann sick like this. But I hated to wait even one more day to see this baby. As soon as it was light, I called the doctor, who was also our friend. He had grown up in this community and had come back to help his people. We liked and respected him and he had already helped us in many ways. I had talked to him the day before to get advice about the baby.

When I told him about Lee Ann's temperature, he said, "I'm coming over. This is an important day for you." He examined her thoroughly and said it looked like the current virus. She'd be better in a couple of days. I was still feeling pulled in two directions by my need to be with Lee Ann and my need to see the baby. The doctor said he'd be around all day. He urged me to ask Jean if she could stay with Lee Ann until we got back. Without his insistence I don't know if I could have left Lee Ann. But Jean came, we found a sitter for her children, and good to his word, the doctor checked in every couple of hours.

To say that this was a happy baby would have been an understatement. He was absolutely exuberant, a big, healthy-looking 10-week old. We took turns holding him and playing with him. I was terribly excited. It was almost too good to believe. The foster mother was in an adjoining room. Peg didn't want him to be away from the mother he knew, so she had asked her to come for this visit. When it was nearly time for his nap, she took him to the foster mother and they left.

We talked to Peg. She gave us the family medical history. She told us that, contrary to current thinking—which was that if you made a child secure enough he would not need to know about his background, and if you knew those things you would unconsciously look for them—she thought that when this baby grew up he would need to know about his family and the reason for the adoption.

She told us they had known both the mother and the father, who had made a very hard decision not to marry at this time. The mother had made sure she had good medical care and nutrition, had brought the baby to Neighborhood House herself, and was prepared to sign the legal papers.

I had a very positive feeling about this young woman whose identity we would never know. Peg told us about the baby's experiences in the foster home, where he'd been part of a happy active family with four children. Then she left the room so we could think in privacy.

We talked together about what a wonderful baby he was, how scared and excited we were, and yes, about how very much we wanted this baby. When Peg returned, she assured us we didn't have to decide right away. But we'd already decided. All that was needed now was to discuss the details of the legal forms, and to make a list of sizes and formula supplies so we could shop for the necessities.

We agreed to come and pick up the baby on Thursday if Lee Ann had a normal temperature on Wednesday. Then we called home to tell her and Jean about how wonderful and cute our baby was. On the way home, I was anxious to get back to Lee Ann quickly. I was worried that, as much as she had wanted us to come, she might interpret our leaving her today as a greater interest in the baby than in her.

On the way home we talked about names. Finally I suggested using the one the baby's biological mother had chosen. The name would be a gift from her, and it was one we liked as well. Paul agreed, and so we decided to call our baby Stephen. For a middle name we chose Paul.

Lee Ann seemed almost recovered the next morning, so I kept her home from school a second day just to be sure. We called to confirm that our decision to take this baby was still the same, and we made arrangements to pick him up on Thursday. With Jean's help I secured the necessities, and with great excitement, we transformed the guest room into a nursery. When we got to Neighborhood House, Lee Ann was so excited she didn't even take time to find her friends. She had brought the pink bunny. "I want to give this to the baby. Let's go see the baby."

As she had the other day, Peg brought Stephen directly from the foster mother, who was in another room, and handed him to me, explaining in a soft voice what was happening. He was wide awake. Lee Ann jumped up and down. "Can I hold him?" She sat down in a large chair and I put him in her lap. "See, new brother, I brought you a bunny." He was dressed in a little white suit and a sweater and a cap and had a blanket his birth mother had given to him. The foster mother had sent us a box with a few clean diapers, a note about feeding, enough formula for the rest of the day, and an envelope of pictures of Stephen at different times over the last 10 weeks. We gave him a bottle in Peg's office and then carried him to the car. We put him in the car bed and Lee Ann climbed in next to him. He looked at her with interest, and then slept almost all the way home.

At home, as late afternoon approached, he began to cry. I knew he sensed not only that we were not his familiar people, but probably that we were inexperienced people as well. Nothing seemed to work, so he cried and we walked. Finally he took a bottle and I put him in his bed. I was exhausted and more than a little shaken. I knew that he was expecting to be comforted in his foster mother's ways, and I didn't know what they were. He slept until the middle of the night and went back to sleep after a bottle.

He was awake at 6:00 A.M., and Lee Ann, hearing him, came down too. The dog was very interested, and would position himself in front of the stroller or securely over the threshold of the door as a protector. Stephen's uneasiness with us could not dampen his wonderful enthusiasm for life, and slowly we learned to comfort him.

Lee Ann's adjustment to the baby was much smoother than I had expected. She loved showing him off, and she liked sharing her knowledge about taking care of babies. She enjoyed his active interest in her. She did become mildly angry when she wanted me to take her somewhere and we couldn't go because the baby was sleeping, or she wanted me to do something with her when he was having a bottle or a diaper change. One day when she was home with yet another virus and I was running back and forth between them, I heard her singing, "Babies are fun, but babies are trouble."

The people in our parishes and our friends went out of their way to be attentive to Lee Ann. Neighbors invited her to play. A special older friend invited her to sit with her at church. Jean, Bob, John, and Bonnie asked her to supper at their house, and church members brought gifts not only to the baby but to Lee Ann as well. She enjoyed all of these special treats and invitations.

Lee Ann, of course, still needed much attention. I was grateful for her days at school, so I could give Stephen my undivided attention. We could enjoy bath time, a stroller ride, or an unrushed feeding. He began to sleep through the night and to go to bed about six o'clock. That meant that when Paul was away in the evenings, I had time to help Lee Ann with homework, or to do special things, and to read to her before bedtime. At the times in the late afternoons or early mornings and weekends when they were both needing things, when Lee Ann got upset, Stephen did too, and his crying and hers were hard for me to manage. I often wished I were two people.

Finally, one day while she was impatiently waiting for me to finish changing his diaper, I said, "You know, I didn't do this for you. I hope whoever did it was loving to you. But I do lots of other things for you that big children like you need, like making doll clothes and reading big-girl books and baking cookies."

My parents came to visit for Stephen's baptism and declared him wonderful. Lee Ann was very comfortable with them, and they were pleased to see the progress she was making. My father was concerned about the effect the decision to stay where we could keep Lee Ann was having on Paul's vocational choices. But he understood our feelings about that issue, and told me that he had made a change in his will which would include both children.

We were becoming more anxious about the future. It was already May, and Paul still had no job for the fall. The loss of control we felt created lots of angry feelings. Until we had some specific possibilities, Peg could not even approach Mr. Steinkohler with the idea of taking Lee Ann out of this state.

Then Paul got a letter from a campus ministry in a town in the Midwest. The letter described the community as a small university town, with both a state university and a small private college. The job opening was for a director of the Westminster Foundation, which served students from both campuses. The chairman of the committee asked him to call to set up an interview.

When Paul returned from the interview the next weekend, he was enthusiastic about the job and the town. He especially liked the people he had met—the campus ministry board, the faculty and students who had been invited to meet him, and the assistant director, whose name was Gail. They were interviewing several people and would get back to him in a few days.

There was lots to think about. Neither of us had ever lived in the Midwest. But having grown up in the South and the East, respectively, and having lived in Kansas, Pennsylvania, and New York City, we assumed we would adjust. The work would be with people very different from those we'd worked with in our present community. But we both enjoyed the college students at summer camp. Paul felt at home in the world of ideas. In a college town he could find the intellectual stimulation he enjoyed. We were both interested in what the church called social action. Maybe we could help students to experience different cultures and confront new ideas. College was a good time to do this.

When the board chairman called to offer Paul the job, Paul reminded him of our commitment to Lee Ann and explained he needed time to work it out. They were willing to wait.

Peg had already talked to Mr. Steinkohler about this once, when Paul first went for the interview. Mr. Steinkohler wanted time to think about it, but he was not totally closed. She called him again to say we definitely wanted to take Lee Ann, that the staff at Neighborhood House felt this was Lee Ann's best choice, and that if he did not agree, they really had no other good alternative for her. She laid out the conditions—that we had agreed to take her on a free home basis (no longer supported financially by Neighborhood House), that we would bring her to visit him at his request as often as he had seen her in the most frequent year (three times), and that she would be supervised by the local county. He still did not know if he could agree.

Meanwhile, Peg set in motion the paperwork required by the welfare department in the county to which we were moving. There were no problems at that end. She also called a former Neighborhood House staff member, who had known Lee Ann at two and who now taught at the small college, in case we needed additional help.

Peg called Mr. Steinkohler every few days. First he thought it would be OK. Then he said he couldn't do it. We were feeling completely powerless and very frustrated. We all believed that Lee Ann's father wanted what was best for her, that he was unable to care for her and didn't really want to, but that he didn't want to lose control. Finally he came in to talk to the staff and agreed to sign a statement giving his permission for the move. Paul called and accepted the job.

At this point we told Lee Ann that we were planning to move to the town Daddy had visited, and that her father had agreed for her to go with us. She asked if Stephen had permission too. We explained that because his parents were unable to take care of him, we were going to adopt him and be his parents. Because she had a father who wanted to be in contact with her, it was not possible for us to adopt her now. She partially understood, but for the first time, the issue of different legal relationships in our family had been raised.

Every time she talked about the move, she began by saying, "We are not leaving this brown house. When do we move? I don't believe I will be able to go with you." We all agreed it was a good sign that she didn't want to leave easily. But nothing I did or said changed her feeling that her life with us was about to fall apart.

Because Stephen was sick and I had to stay home with him, Lee Ann and Paul went to look at the new house and make final arrangements. She came back having met lots of new people and said, "Everyone there seems to be adopted." Paul said that the people next door and the campus minister we were replacing had adopted children. Lee Ann felt good about this.

We spent the summer enjoying the students who helped in the day camp and saying good-bye to good friends. These were days of great ambivalence. Our work here had been meaningful. We had learned a lot, and we hoped we had helped others.

My parents came to help us pack and move. Lee Ann became more and more anxious as the packing began. Any little thing that happened made her angry. She was upset when we took the pictures down. Finally, moving day arrived. She was still uncertain she was coming with us, and she saw to it her things were in separate boxes. Finally her bicycle went into the van and a favorite stuffed animal into the seat of Granddaddy's car. At that point she began to trust that it was going to be OK, and she ran up and down the street saying good-bye to neighbors. "My whole family is moving, and I'm going too."

We moved in, went off on a vacation, and then came back to settle in. There were lots of good things for Lee Ann. The Baptist campus minister had a daughter her age and in her class at school. They became friends. I had raised the issue, both as we left her old school and when we registered her at the new one, about the possibility of catching up in school by placing her in fourth rather than fifth grade. Everyone agreed that it would damage her already shaky self-confidence, so we didn't.

I was delighted with her teacher, a lovely young woman who liked Lee Ann and helped her in many ways to feel comfortable. The work we'd done over many months seemed to come together. In this exciting classroom she was finally reading fluently and was pleased with herself.

The neighborhood was great for all of us. When Bill and Sarah next door came back from vacation, they included us in the spontaneous neighborhood picnics, potluck suppers, and ladies' nights at the movies. Paul played tennis with Bill and others in the English Department. Their yard and ours ran together and there was a picnic table on the edge where we brought coffee out in the late mornings for a few minutes and chatted with other neighbors. We felt at home right away.

After a few weeks, it was clear that if we wanted to see Paul much, we would have to find ways to be involved with his work. I missed these experiences anyway. We began to take the children to the Sunday night student suppers and to have groups of students and families to dinner at our house. We usually invited people to bring their children for informal meals. We often did things with Gail, Paul's colleague. She was unmarried and liked having children around. She was wonderful at helping me feel included.

Having made this move with us, Lee Ann seemed to feel more secure in our family. The terrible apprehension about being sent back because of her behavior was largely gone, and she was more relaxed and happy than she had been. She enjoyed Stephen and played happily with friends. Little things didn't seem to bother her so much. Stephen still went to bed early, so we had the evenings for reading or games or homework. In her extra 30 minutes after bedtime, Lee Ann was rereading children's classics we had read to her.

At the time we moved, Mr. Steinkohler had wanted our telephone number. Neighborhood House still mostly communicated with him for us. But he began to call us, and that was something new. At first they were friendly calls. Then one night when he called he seemed to have had too much to drink. He quizzed Lee Ann about her knowledge of the Bible. He rebuked me for neglecting her religious training, then hung up abruptly.

Once he called in a fine mood to tell me about something he was leaving Lee Ann in his will. Then one night, when we had left the children with a baby-sitter, the phone rang while the sitter was upstairs taking care of Stephen. Lee Ann answered, "Lindsays. Lee Ann speaking."

A voice shouted, "Lee Ann who?"

"The Lindsay's Lee Ann."

"No, you're not! You're Lee Ann Steinkohler! I'll come get you and teach you how to answer the phone!"

Lee Ann threw the phone down and ran straight to Sarah's house next door. Not able to tell Sarah what was wrong, she was still sitting on her lap sobbing and shaking when we arrived home.

We talked a long time that night. Lee Ann told us it was OK to see her father at Neighborhood House, but other times she was very scared of him. She said she never knew if he would be friendly or mad, or why he was that way. We told her how to answer the phone without identifying herself. We also decided to use an older, more experienced baby-sitter.

It was several weeks until she seemed as secure as she had been before. She apparently was less scared that we would disapprove of her, but more afraid that her father would come get her or in some way upset the balance.

Stephen continued to grow from baby to little boy with his own strong personality. He began to walk and talk. The first name he said was "Yee Ann," which showed how important she was to him. It certainly did not seem that Mr. Steinkohler would lose interest in Lee Ann and agree to her adoption. I felt threatened by his calls and became worried about what might happen to Stephen if Lee Ann ever had to go back to her father. How would he ever understand his life with us as secure?

When the new county social worker made her visit, I discussed this with her. We wanted to adopt another baby anyway, and hoped also, with a second adoption, to reinforce Stephen's sense of permanence. The social worker said we weren't eligible for an infant since there was a shortage of adoptable babies and we already had two children. I tried to explain that until Lee Ann could be adopted her father could take her back any time, so we really didn't have two children, but she didn't seem to understand. She was young and inexperienced, and I doubted her ability to handle our unusual situation sympathetically.

I called the director of the agency and explained our situation again. He agreed we needed a highly skilled social worker. We were reassigned to Mrs. Brown, who had just come back into the office after raising her family. We liked her immediately. This was a new kind of case, but she was willing to try. She was also willing to discuss an adoption application for a baby with the director.

At spring break we took a group of students to Kentucky to a work camp. All of us, including Stephen, slept on sleeping bags on the floor of the church. The students responded positively to the people they met and contributed a significant amount of work to this community. On the way to the work camp, our family visited horse farms and historic places, and Lee Ann wrote a paper to take back to school.

Lee Ann's life at school was improving day by day. She got along well with the other children. In our neighborhood she made the acquaintance of a new girl, Lisa, whose mother had died. Lisa was adjusting to her new stepmother, a warm and sensitive woman. She and Lee Ann had a lot in common, and Lisa became Lee Ann's first self-chosen best friend.

Stephen was able to move about rapidly now, and sometimes he got into things Lee Ann didn't want him to have. While there was more friction than before, the relationship between them was still warm and loving. Stephen had been with us a year now, and with the help of a local attorney, we scheduled the final adoption hearing. Lee Ann went with us. We made it clear to her that she was an important part of the family adopting Stephen.

When summer came, our third with Lee Ann, we took a group of eight students to Cleveland for seven weeks. The students worked in the neighborhood center that our former colleague Bob was directing. They took a puppet theater into the parks and streets and directed recreation for children. They became acquainted with each other and with the community in which they were working. The two boys lived with our family in one apartment and the girls lived in an apartment across the hall.

Except for the few white students with us, we were the only white people in an inner city housing area. It was safe because of a fence and a guard, but outside this redeveloped project was a slum. Lee Ann went to a morning summer program at Western Reserve's lab school. While she was gone, Stephen and I did the food shopping for the day at a neighborhood supermarket. A friendly produce person saved special pieces of fruit for Stephen.

Lee Ann usually came in happy after an exciting morning with other children. After Stephen's nap, we spent many afternoons in Bob and Jean's fenced-in yard about 15 minutes away. Other days we toured museums or parks. Lee Ann could not get enough of the health museum. At last, here were some answers to her questions about the human body. Sometimes the children played outside with children from nearby apartments, and then we ate dinner with the students. We enjoyed being with Bob and Jean and liked working with the students. Living in an apartment with students, eating every meal with a group, adjusting to the frantic pace and danger of this part of the city, and being responsible for so many people made it an intense summer.

We had not heard from Mr. Steinkohler in some time, and he had not requested a visit through Neighborhood House. The staff at Neighborhood House had decided that since the service project was in the state where we lived, we did not need to get permission from Mr. Steinkohler. Each time we needed to make such a decision, it reminded us that much of Lee Ann's life was decided elsewhere, and though we were always listened to carefully, the decisions were not ours.

On our way home we went to visit Neighborhood House. Peg arranged a visit with Mr. Steinkohler. It was similar to previous visits. He did not mention the phone calls and we didn't either. When Peg told us she was getting married and leaving Neighborhood House, we were upset. Peg was the person who had made everything possible. Fortunately, Janet would be able to work with us. Peg assured us that she would handle our situation well. When we visited with Janet and talked to her at length, we were impressed with the scope of her knowledge and how well she understood the details of Lee Ann's situation. It was a relief to know we were still in competent hands.

From there we went to a family camp near my parents' home. We spent a week in several cabins with cousins, aunts, uncles, my sister and her fiancé, and several families who worked for my Dad. Lee Ann loved being with all these people. They were interested in her and she had lots of fun. She had her first horseback ride. Because her swimming skills were so strong, she wanted to water ski like the grownups. One of the people from my Dad's company dragged her behind the boat all afternoon. She wouldn't give up. He said, "I knew she was either going to ski or drown!" Luckily she skied, and we all learned something about persistence.

Everything at home seemed green, quiet, and calm after the frantic pace of the summer. Lee Ann was glad to see Lisa, who spent most afternoons at our house. The two girls raked big piles of leaves and let Stephen play in the leaves with them. They took him on rides around the neighborhood in his wagon, and, in an early snow, pulled him up and down the sidewalk on the sled.

Lee Ann was glad to be back with her friends at school, but almost immediately I knew something was wrong. Instead of the relaxed, happy homecoming from school of last spring, she was usually angry and out of sorts. She was annoyed with Stephen, short-tempered with me, and uncommunicative about her days.

As the fall progressed, Lee Ann had a harder time getting up for school. We tried to explore her feelings about sixth grade. She told me it was hard, and that her friends from last year only wanted to be friends when they were mad at each other. I knew there had been few invitations to spend the night or to play after school, and it became clear that she rushed home from school not only to play with Lisa, but also to escape from an uncomfortable situation.

I talked to the sixth grade teacher in mid-October. She was aware that Lee Ann was feeling "out of it" with the class. Even though her summer school had strengthened her academic skills, she was still far behind her classmates.

She was quiet and didn't participate verbally in the class activities. And, yes, what she said about the friends was true. They were a particularly sophisticated group of sixth graders, and over the summer their interests had changed to clothes and music and talk about boys. Lee Ann's eleventh birthday was approaching, but many of the girls would be 12 in a few weeks. A growth spurt through the summer meant that she was no longer much smaller than other sixth graders. She was developing physically and becoming more of a young woman. But even with her increased height and physical development, she wasn't in the same place as the other girls.

"What can we do?" I asked the teacher.

She said she really didn't know what to suggest.

"What if we gave her another year to mature before starting junior high?"

The teacher was adamant. It was against school policy and therefore impossible. Holding Lee Ann back would damage her self-esteem. She refused to even consider the idea.

I left the conference feeling confused. Up to this point, I had always felt that the schools and the family were working together for the benefit of my child. It was true the teacher cared; she would do all she could to help Lee Ann achieve academically, and she would try to help her be accepted socially. But there were no offers of creative thinking, and standing school policy seemed to cut off one possible option.

Frustrated with the school's response, we decided more information might help us figure out a way to help Lee Ann. The school had done group testing, but because of the difficult emotional issues she was dealing with, neither they nor we felt the results were accurate. We arranged to have individual diagnostic testing done by a private psychologist, to see if we could pinpoint some of the learning problems.

The results were inconclusive. They showed that Lee Ann had at least average intelligence. However, she still had so many emotional problems interfering with her performance that there was no way to get an accurate assessment. Lee Ann's active curiosity and her ability to learn quickly had already convinced me that her ability was higher than the tests showed. We decided to focus on the emotional obstacles. The psychologist was available for play therapy, so we asked her to work with Lee Ann.

We explained to Lee Ann what she could expect, and, while she wasn't wildly enthusiastic, she wasn't negative either. She went dutifully to meet with the therapist for an hour every Saturday, but said very little about how it was going. Nevertheless we hoped the therapy would help us all to understand the problems and feelings Lee Ann was having in school and in her life.

There were other signs that beneath the surface all was not well. We received telephone calls and several letters from Lee Ann's father. Sometimes he was in a good mood, but often he was angry about something—it was impossible to know what. Since someone wrote the letters for him, it was even difficult to know if these were his own thoughts. There were no specific messages for Lee Ann, but she talked to him on the phone and she was aware of the letters.

The phone calls were especially upsetting to Lee Ann. Each time it was as much as two weeks before she recovered her equilibrium. She spent a lot of time just sitting in a rigid posture. Little things made her angry. Her talk about herself was more often, "Nothing good ever happens to me."

I had trouble knowing what to do with my angry feelings about these calls. We worked hard to give Lee Ann experiences that would increase her confidence and her sense of security within our family. But a five-minute conversation with her father was devastating to her fragile sense of self-worth. It was obvious that I couldn't respond to him in anger. That would increase his negative response and jeopardize Lee Ann's security even more. I couldn't say anything negative to Lee Ann about her father. She had to relate to him, no matter what, and she was already ambivalent at best.

The social workers were supportive, but they, too, had to maintain some neutrality to be of help to Lee Ann. Talking to friends wasn't helpful. They mostly said things like "Why do you put up with that?" or "I don't know how you do it." Paul and I talked to each other about our feelings of being caught in a no-win situation. But mostly, I just raged to myself, knowing it was unfair, but that I was powerless to prevent the calls. There was nothing I could do that wouldn't jeopardize something I cared more about. A week or two after each call, Lee Ann regained her confidence and our life together was calmer again.

Overall, though, at school and at home, things continued to deteriorate. Lee Ann was having temper tantrums like the ones she had when she first came to us, over small issues—the tightness of the socks, the forgotten homework, the improperly ironed dress. They always ended with her saying, "Nothing good ever happens to me," and now she added, "You love Stephen more because he is part of your family forever and I'm not."

The tantrums frequently came in the morning as she struggled to get dressed for school. They were directed at anyone nearby—Paul, Stephen, or me—and often ran their course too late to walk to school. As before, we insisted when she pulled herself together that she keep to her routine, and I drove her to school late. Sometimes the tantrums erupted at night, and delayed sleep for everyone, making us all tired the next day. We tried to talk with Lee Ann about her feelings after things were calm or at other times, but she could express them only with great agitation. It was hard to know what she felt.

At school, she continued to be withdrawn, avoiding participation in many of the activities. The one positive connection in Lee Ann's life outside our family at that point was her friendship with Lisa. They talked and enjoyed doing things together.

During the Christmas vacation, we went to stay with my parents for the wedding of my sister. Lee Ann showed more enthusiasm about the preparations for our trip than she had for anything else all fall. I made a new dress for her to wear. The two weeks away from home were a vacation in many ways. The tension of school was gone. Here in our extended family she could be the little girl again, accepted just because she was Lee Ann. She enjoyed the attention, relaxed, and was much easier to live with. As a result Paul and I were able to relax too.

The good feelings lasted through the first couple of weeks back at home. Then the temper tantrums returned, with increasing frequency. It now seemed forever since Lee Ann had expressed anything positive. I got out my child development books to see what they had to say about early adolescence. Everything we were seeing was indeed part of this stage: conflicting needs for both dependence and independence, the sudden changes of mood, the need for privacy, expressions of extreme emotion. Nonetheless, it was clear that what we were experiencing was unusually intense.

When I called the therapist to see what insights she could offer, she said she didn't know why Lee Ann was so upset, because she didn't talk about her feelings in the therapy sessions. She told me to tell Lee Ann to talk to her. This statement made me wonder if the psychologist was qualified to do play therapy. She should be observing Lee Ann's play and talking to her about it. It certainly was not my role to tell Lee Ann to talk. The therapist told me she thought that Lee Ann should not play with Lisa so much because Lisa was younger (about a year) and not in her class at school. I told the therapist that didn't make sense to me. This was a meaningful relationship, her first self-chosen best friend, probably the only person she was sharing feelings with, and a very responsible girl.

Lee Ann would be 11 on the 31st of January. She was busily planning her party. I hoped, and I think she did too, that having the friends from her class in our home once more would set in motion the happy relationships we had enjoyed last spring. She decided on a movie party. We looked through the rental catalog and she picked out an old Lucille Ball movie. She sent her invitations, and she and Lisa spent several happy afternoons making red and white striped bags for popcorn.

On the day of the party, Lee Ann was excited and happy. She graciously accepted the brightly wrapped packages as her friends arrived. It was good to see her smile. As the girls sat down to eat supper, instead of the group experience I expected, they divided into two or sometimes three groups of giggling, whispering friends. Lee Ann was never included in any of these groups. During the movie it was apparent from the comments and loud laughing that they thought the movie more silly than funny. Again, Lee Ann and Lisa were isolated, not able to figure out what was going on. The girls threw popcorn around the room and when the movie was over they left in a noisy group.

The party helped me understand more fully the problems of earning social acceptance in the sixth grade.

I worried about a lot of things that year. I remembered the question Daddy asked me when we decided to take Lee Ann: "What if you become attached and you can't have a positive relationship, and she makes you miserable?" Was this happening now? Would it ever be any different? Would the anger ever go away? How would we survive? How would Lee Ann survive? What kind of person would she become?

I worried about Stephen too. What was it like to grow up around so much intense, negative emotion, with some of it directed at him? How would he ever feel secure if we lost Lee Ann? How would he know it couldn't happen to him? Had we made a mistake to try this? At times it seemed not only difficult, but impossible.

Only one thing was clear and not in question—we were not going to give up. Lee Ann had the power to hurt us all, but we were working hard to take care of ourselves and Stephen, and underneath the absolute discouragement, I hoped that we could survive as a family.

All of Lee Ann's volatile feelings built up into one night of a dreadful temper tantrum, triggered by frustration with a homework assignment. Then she couldn't find her favorite stuffed animal, and was sure that Stephen had taken it. There was no bread for cinnamon toast, and off she went. I sent her to her room to calm down, and for 45 minutes we could hear the shouting and yelling, punctuated by, "Nothing good ever happens...Nothing good ever happens..."

Finally she became somewhat calmer. I went in to talk about what was really bothering her. She talked about school, people who were mean, how hard the work was, and that on a recent visit with her father she felt she didn't even know him. "You see," she said, "nothing good ever

happens, and you don't love me as much as Stephen because you adopted him and he will be with you forever."

That was the last straw for me. "After all we've done
together, Lee Ann, if you don't know I love you, I don't
know what to say. We want to adopt you. We want you to
be with us forever. There is no possible way to make this
happen now. I can't do it. Janet can't do it. There is nothing more we can do." I knew I was shouting and I didn't
care. "If you don't know I love you, I guess you never will."
I was so upset I left the room to calm down.

After a while I went back into her room, where she
was still sobbing, and we talked about her feelings of being different from kids at school and even from Stephen
in our family. I assured her of our love and our desire to
adopt her, and explained that her father would have to
agree to the adoption. "Then I'm going to ask him," she
said. "I want to be here always."

The next day I called Janet to explain how bad things
had become and to discuss our need to try to work out an
adoption now. If her father could take care of her, it would
be better to resolve it now. If he couldn't, we needed to
have her permanence with us assured. I wanted his contact with her to be assured too. Janet said they had been
consistently losing in the local court. They were working
hard for new laws, but the courts were not a promising
way to go. Finally, together, we worked out a plan whereby
Lee Ann could go for a long visit, maybe staying with her
father and grandfather, so they could think about their
relationship. Then maybe Janet could help them work out
an adoption voluntarily.

Though Lee Ann did not understand the reasons why
adults could not take care of her needs, she was willing to
do anything that might make adoption possible. She said
that it would be scary to visit her father, but she would

like to do it. Meanwhile, I was feeling that most things in my life were out of control.

In late March, we took a group of students to Kentucky for a work camp. We stayed in a cabin at a children's home and worked on their buildings. The atmosphere of the children's home—the dining hall, the group activities of the children—reminded Lee Ann of Neighborhood House and triggered upsetting feelings. She had some positive interactions with at least one child, but I noticed a lot of anger. When it was her turn to push the playground merry-go-round, she did it jerkily and too fast so that the little children almost fell off. She dragged her feet getting dressed in the morning and arrived sullenly at breakfast. Her answers to questions were usually a curt yes or no. I considered driving back home to let her see the therapist, because the feelings were so close to the surface. But that was too complicated. Instead, we talked a lot about what she was feeling. When we got back home, I talked to the therapist, who said, "Oh, I couldn't have seen you then. Her time is Saturday morning." Again, I felt uneasy about this therapist, who wanted her to talk but only at a particular time.

Throughout the spring I continued to talk with the teacher, and then the principal, about Lee Ann's situation. The principal finally agreed that if both we and the teacher thought giving her another year would help, he was willing to try. I told him we wanted to talk to Lee Ann and would make the change only if she was willing.

The teacher and I talked to her, explaining that we understood how hard sixth grade had been for her, and that if she were with people closer to her age with a chance to catch up academically, school might not be so hard. Her initial reaction was, "No!" We let it go, but she took Stephen walking up to the new elementary school that was being built three blocks from us, just to look around. I knew she was talking about this to Lisa, who went to a different school, and, therefore, was not associated with the problems.

I called to discuss the school situation with the therapist, who told me she had no suggestions because Lee Ann still wasn't talking. Almost as an afterthought, she mentioned that she would be gone for two months beginning next week. By this time, I was convinced that she was not a good therapist for Lee Ann and I decided to stop the sessions. While she had probably not done any harm, she had done very little good. I had cause to doubt her skill right from the beginning, but it was difficult for me to trust my observations because she was supposed to be the expert.

Throughout this whole time I was grateful for our friends. When Lee Ann needed to be alone to work out her anger and Paul was working in the basement study, there were several friends I could visit with Stephen for a few moments of calm, ordinary conversation and a cup of tea. I had joined the League of Women Voters and belonged to a committee on local government where everyone brought their children. It was a good outlet for me, and Stephen liked the other children. Church Women United had organized a discussion group of white and black women to discuss our different life experiences. This kept me connected to the community. I planned my days so that the time Lee Ann was in school was a time to do special things with Stephen—have other children over, go to the library, walk uptown. In this way, I could ensure that Lee Ann's problems did not prevent him from having many positive experiences, both time alone with me and time with other children. Stephen, with his ever increasing grasp of language, his wonderful physical energy, and his optimistic view of life, was just the antidote to all the gloom we were experiencing. Most of the time Lee Ann still responded warmly to him, and he was devoted to her.

We were all apprehensive about Lee Ann's visit with her father, which had been scheduled for late July. A few weeks before she went, I talked with Janet. She said she had blocked off time on her calendar to be helpful in any way she could. Also, Dr. Williams, a nearby psychiatrist who gave free time to Neighborhood House, would be available if needed. Janet was having some very tentative discussions about adoption with Mr. Steinkohler.

We hoped the visit would bring some kind of resolution toward making Lee Ann's status permanent. I was afraid of adolescence, with all of its identity problems, unless Lee Ann had a clear sense of where she belonged. Even a permanent life with her father would have been preferable to perpetual uncertainty. On the other hand, letting our child go into a situation she was afraid of, without the comforting presence of the people who she felt were her family, was almost more than I could handle. We felt powerless to protect her from a situation no child should have to face. The lack of control felt terrible.

On the day she was to fly to see her father, Lee Ann woke up with a sore throat. It was obvious from her eyes and her tense body that she was apprehensive about the solo flight and about the visit. But she kept saying, "I want to go." There were no other symptoms, so after consultation with Janet, who was to meet her at the airport, we took her to the plane. Stephen, sensing the tension, cried when she walked to the plane without us.

She had been gone about eight hours when the phone rang. It was Dr. Williams, the psychiatrist. He explained that Lee Ann and Mr. Steinkohler were both in his office. It seemed that 10 minutes after Janet had left Lee Ann to visit with her father and grandfather, Lee Ann had asked her father's permission for the adoption. He immediately became furious, saying he would punish her for saying this by refusing to let her leave the house again. There was such an uproar that a neighbor who was standing by at the request of Janet called her to come back. She did, and brought them to Dr. Williams for help in resolving the conflict.

Dr. Williams told us that Lee Ann had asked him to call us, and she was going to listen as he described their conversation. Lee Ann had talked to him about how hard it is not to have a permanent family. She talked about how she came to us and had no trust that we would allow her to stay very long. She had tried to be very good, and then, finally, she wanted to know what would happen if she wasn't so good. She tried all the things she thought upset grownups, and still she was allowed to stay. And now, she said, she really wanted to stay forever, like Stephen.

She was constantly afraid of having to leave—so much that she couldn't think of anything else. She liked talking with Lisa because her mother had died and she had a new stepmother. She didn't feel so awfully different when she talked to Lisa. She told him how our family had fun together, and it wasn't only her parents and her brother. She had grandparents and an aunt and a great aunt and cousins, and she had to get this worked out because family camp was next week. She had to go to family camp.

"I wish you could have heard how much she loves you, how much a part of your family she feels. You would have been overwhelmed."

"I guess I would," I said. "You see, we haven't heard much of anything positive in the last year."

"Oh, by the way," he said, "she wants to go to the new school with the orange doors."

"I'm surprised you got into that," I said.

"Oh, we've talked about a lot of things. What I want to ask is, could one of you come here? I think to work this out Lee Ann has to go back to her father's house and play a compassionate adult role. I've talked to her a lot about it. She wants to work it out and she thinks she can, if one of you is nearby, even if she can't see you."

"Of course," we both responded. "We'll check on planes. One of us will come in the morning."

"By the way," Dr. Williams asked, "is Stephen still up? Lee Ann wants to talk to him."

On our end, we heard Stephen say, "Yee Ann, you come on home." Then we talked to her and told her one of us would be there tomorrow, and that we loved her.

Paul was to go to a campus ministry conference the next day. My parents agreed to look after Stephen at their house, and Paul could take him down there. I prepared to fly to Lee Ann. Janet called to say she would meet my plane. Peg would be on vacation and had offered me her house.

By the time I arrived I was emotionally exhausted. I was afraid that we had set in motion a catastrophe for us all. But I also had hope that Mr. Steinkohler's intentions would become clear and that a permanent placement for Lee Ann would now be possible.

Janet took me to Peg's house and then caught me up on what was happening. It seemed that when he was calmer and had thought about it, Mr. Steinkohler decided he really didn't want Lee Ann to spend the nights at his house. Maybe after breakfast until dinner time would be enough. I wondered if Mr. Steinkohler, after dealing with Lee Ann when she was almost as angry as he was, had begun to think about how difficult it would be to actually live with her. Janet said she had decided that Lee Ann should spend the nights at Neighborhood House, but would bring her here first.

After a tearful reunion, Lee Ann and I spent the evening talking about her feelings and how difficult and frightening her father was. She thought the day had been OK. Mr. Steinkohler didn't pay much attention to her, but she had visited with her grandfather. Janet told Lee Ann about events in her father's life that had made him such an angry person. She left with the assurance that I would be right here and that she would see me tomorrow.

Lee Ann had several appointments with Dr. Williams, and spent most of the days at her father's. In between we visited and went to a movie. It seemed to me she had a new self-confidence. She was doing something difficult and getting through the days. In addition, she didn't need to ask if I would stay as long as necessary or if she could count on Janet. For the first time she was able to trust our commitment to her, and her idea of what she wanted never wavered.

I asked if I could talk to Dr. Williams, and that was arranged. His first remark to me was, "I took a big chance when I called you. I was so afraid you wouldn't come, and I was also afraid that if you did come, you would be smothering and not able to let us do what we had to do. I'm glad that neither of those things happened."

I liked him immediately. He was a very warm, welcoming, including kind of person, easy to talk to.

"By the way," he asked, "when did Lee Ann become a Lindsay?"

Surprised, I started to tell him about the mixed-up legal situation.

He said, "No, I mean, when did she begin to feel like a Lindsay? It really is not the usual thing for a foster child to make such a tight connection."

I told him that it was a surprise to learn that Lee Ann felt anything positive toward us; all we'd heard for months were our many faults. We decided that was partly normal adolescent behavior, partly Lee Ann's own problems.

"But," he said, "she really does feel loved and cared about and part of your whole extended family."

I asked him how he had gotten so far with her in a few days when she hadn't talked to the therapist at home in five months. He said that at a time of crisis, everything is on the surface. Also, she had come to the place where the problems with her father started and where he was. He offered to help her father work out his relationship with Lee Ann.

He continued, "In cases with foster children, it often is unclear what solution is best. But in this case, it is clear that adoption is what we should work for. Lee Ann is sure that adoption is what she wants. She feels very much a part of your family. I hope I can work with the father to help him make the decision she wants, but it will take time. I think he will soon understand that he really cannot take care of Lee Ann. Probably the court would not let him. But he might be able to have her brought back to this state for another impermanent placement."

As the days went on, Mr. Steinkohler began to lose interest in Lee Ann's visits. He requested she be brought later and picked up earlier. Lee Ann began to spend more and more time at Neighborhood House, talking with the social workers, visiting with the kids, and especially visiting with Momma Miller, who had been the housemother when Lee Ann was younger. Despite the fact that it was a new building with a different purpose—it was a residential treatment center for children now—this was a return to her roots, a reclaiming of some good things from her past.

I had been in close contact by phone with my parents and Stephen. He told me about picking little baby lima beans at Great Nanna's, playing in the playhouse, watering Granddaddy's flowers. Every conversation included, "Where's Yee-Ann?" I knew he was being loved and cared for in the best ways, but I also knew I needed to be with him again. Lee Ann was more relaxed, and Mr. Steinkohler now seemed to assume she would return to our home. It was all right to leave.

When I left, Lee Ann was OK. She felt sure she would be coming to family camp in a few days. But since everything depended on Mr. Steinkohler's decision, anything was possible. I was tremendously relieved five days later when her plane touched down at the local airport, and Stephen was ecstatic to see his sister.

When Lee Ann arrived, she looked so confident that she almost seemed taller. She had handled a difficult situation and gotten at least part of what she wanted, which was to be here at camp with all her family. My sister Ann and her husband were at the camp with their greyhound dog. Lee Ann could not stop laughing when the dog got so upset at being abandoned in the cabin while we went to dinner that he ate Ann's bathing suit, leaving not a shred. This became one of Lee Ann's stored-up memories. She water-skied, rode horses, kibitzed, and learned to play bridge. As for me, I was relieved and exhausted and loved having some time to recuperate.

When we came home, at the end of that summer when Lee Ann was 11, things were much the same. She still was with us as a foster child. Her father was refusing to consider adoption, and we still had no control over that decision. Lee Ann was still an early adolescent with changes of mood, uncertain whether she was child or woman. She still didn't readily express positive feelings.

But in another way, everything had changed. She trusted that we loved her and would be there when she needed us, that nothing she would do or think or say could change that. Even though there was no permanent legal arrangement, the emotional bond was strong and would not change. Both she and we considered her a full member of our family.

Lee Ann's willingness to risk sharing some of her more private thoughts was an indication of her newfound ability to trust. Even though, from my point of view, we had achieved far less in assuring her permanence than we had hoped, it seemed that if Mr. Steinkohler were going to make good on his threat to remove her, he would have done so while she was there.

Janet had explained to him that the placement with us was, in their opinion, in Lee Ann's best interest. If he did not accept this, then they could have nothing more to do with caring for her. We all felt that he really wanted what was best for her, and that if the court had forced him to give her up for adoption, he would have been relieved. But somehow he couldn't make this decision voluntarily.

As we continued to wrestle with these experiences of the summer, Lee Ann began attending the new neighborhood school with the orange doors. I fully expected she would be ambivalent about her decision to repeat sixth grade, and angry with us when things did not go well. But it didn't happen that way. She was much more comfortable with this class. Not only were they her age, but, by chance, they were also less sophisticated. She had an imaginative teacher who made learning activities so interesting that her self-confidence increased.

As weeks went by and things continued to go well at school, I began to think about why. First, it was extremely important that with our help and Dr. Williams', Lee Ann had participated in the decision to change schools. I believe that, had this been a decision imposed by the school, it would have damaged her self-esteem. Second, it helped that the new school was separate from the place where her former classmates were. In addition, Lee Ann's teacher wanted her to succeed, and she made a special effort to be helpful and show Lee Ann that she cared about her. The teacher invited her to come to her barn across the road from us to visit her horses. She brought books from the school library she thought Lee Ann would like, and she offered special help with math.

I began to understand also that my attitude toward schools had been naive. I had expected they would automatically have my child's best interest in mind in any decision they made about her. I began to think about the different roles parents and teacher play in a child's life, and I knew I had to be the advocate for her interests. In this decision, we had finally helped the school to treat our child individually, to open up the possibility that her present rate of achievement might not be the potential rate and that more could be done about it.

Lee Ann was beginning to read everything she could find about horses. Her experience riding at family camp had sparked her interest. We arranged for her to have lessons at the local stable. She could ride her bike to the barn, and she spent many hours there.

She also enjoyed dropping in at the campus ministry house and talking to Paul or Gail or the students who were around. She joined a Girl Scout troop that included her new sixth-grade classmates. Sadly, the first meeting was the kind of experience I always dreaded. One of the leaders lectured her publicly about being a foster child, saying that she had worked with another such child who was lazy, and that Lee Ann would have to work hard to fit in.

Before Lee Ann got home, another leader called to tell me what happened so I would be prepared. She said she was so angry she was going to resign. I said, "Don't. We need you."

When Lee Ann came home she was tearful, and we talked. She told me how embarrassed she felt. "There was no excuse for the leader's behavior," I assured her. "She must be a very mixed up person."

When the offending leader called, I couldn't think of anything to say. She began by saying, "If I had known she was your child... If I had known her father was a minister...." I finally ended the conversation with, "Thank you for calling."

Despite the terrible beginning, Lee Ann loved Girl Scouts. She and a friend from her class did lots of camping activities, and by mid-winter, she was looking forward to Girl Scout summer camp.

After the first Girl Scout meeting, I was reluctant to put any information on the camp form that could be used in a negative way, so I didn't. This time, however, I got a call from her camp counselor, saying, "Lee Ann has made up lots of stories about her early life. I don't know what to do about it." "Unfortunately, they are all true," I answered. This was a difficult issue—deciding what information would be helpful and who we could trust.

That year, when Lee Ann was in sixth grade for the second time, Paul's work was bringing interesting people and issues into our home. Students from many countries offered experiences of geography and culture for both children. Stephen's personal favorite was P.K., a graduate student from India, who stopped by to visit and would tell him folk tales from his country. Students who missed their native foods brought their ingredients to cook in our kitchen, and we shared exotic meals.

The civil rights movement was in full swing. Activists spoke on our campus and came to our house for dinner. Lee Ann's interest in all kinds of people was a special asset. The simplest Appalachian person we met on the work camp and the most highly trained writer were equally valuable to her. Almost everyone responded to Lee Ann and enjoyed her straightforward questions and comments.

Although I felt more secure now about Lee Ann's permanence in our family, the previous summer had been a scary experience. My fears for Stephen's security if something should happen still worried me. What if we were to have another child? At almost three, Stephen was a good age for this. I called and checked with the social worker before we left for Paul's parents' home for Thanksgiving. She said, "No baby yet."

About 10 days after we returned, Mrs. Brown, the county social worker, called. "I have a baby for you. Could you come this afternoon to see him?" When we arrived in her office she was working on some papers at her desk. Asleep in a laundry basket was the baby. She woke him gently. He had big dark eyes and lots of dark hair. He was very calm and didn't mind being disturbed. We held him and visited with him. She said, "You can get him tomorrow afternoon." We were terribly excited, and rushed home to tell Lee Ann, who hadn't heard anything about it because she was at school, and Stephen, who we didn't want to tell until we knew for sure.

I was mildly disturbed by the extreme casualness of this situation. The foster mother wasn't anywhere around. Mrs. Brown had picked him up sometime earlier in the day. But the baby was certainly wonderful.

The four of us went the next afternoon to get our baby. As we passed the large downtown department store, which was decorated for Christmas, Stephen said, "See lights for our baby!" Lee Ann and Stephen were excited, and the baby was just as calm and smiling as he had been the day before—and in the same basket.

Mrs. Brown handed us a sheet of formula and food information and we signed the initial documents. I expected her to tell us more about his background. When she didn't, I asked. She said, "He has no known genetic diseases. Beyond that, it is our policy not to tell you these things. You'll only look for them in the child. He'll become part of your family and he won't need this." I didn't believe her. But I decided this was not the moment to take on agency policy. And so Timothy Martin (for my Dad), two and one-half months, became a very important part of our family.

Part 3

It was a very special Christmas. We spent the holidays with my parents so they could meet their new grandson. Everyone was glad to see Lee Ann and Stephen. Lee Ann's ease with and closeness to my parents were very evident on this visit.

Any displacement Lee Ann had felt with Stephen's arrival was not evident with the new baby. She was enthralled and enjoyed taking care of him. He also benefited from having more experienced parents. Stephen was mostly positive, but he was annoyed when the baby interfered with things that he and I did together. Once he said, "That's a very nice baby you brought here, but I live at 406 East Oak Street, and he better find himself another address." I was able to get a baby-sitter occasionally in the morning so we could still do things together, and because Stephen took an early afternoon nap, there was time alone with the baby. But life was busy.

For her twelfth birthday, Lee Ann had a successful party with bowling and make-your-own-sundaes. She invited her new less sophisticated sixth grade classmates and her old friend Lisa. All of the guests had a good time together, and they included Lee Ann and Lisa in their giggling, happy conversation.

Meanwhile, we had received permission from the campus ministry board to use the money they had been paying for our rent to buy a house. We had been looking for several months, and finally, in the spring, we bought a lot. There was a ravine in the back and a creek at the bottom of the hill. The woods were alive with blooming dogtooth violets. The developers were two professors who made the lots available to people of any race and put aside some land for neighborhood recreation. We hired an architect from the university who liked projects that he and his students could do together, so the cost of building was about the same as that of buying a house. The neighborhood was congenial. Bill and Sarah had plans to build there when they returned from Africa, and several other friends had similar plans. Lee Ann was happy because two students from her sixth grade class would be our neighbors, and the horseback riding stable was nearby.

After the good experience with Dr. Williams in the summer, we knew that professional help would be a support for all of us. We had tried one local person and that had not been helpful. We explored the full range of possibilities and finally concluded that the best help available would be in a city where we went for shopping. We took Lee Ann there to see the allergist twice a year. But the drive of more than an hour made a weekly appointment with a therapist almost out of the question. So we put together what we could: Janet on the telephone, Dr. Williams each time we visited Lee Ann's father, and ministers and counselors who were our friends. One especially supportive woman was a counselor at the university and a colleague of Paul. She had a wise heart and plenty of practical experience. These arrangements, while not perfect, seemed the best we could do where we were.

The next summer, Lee Ann went back for another visit with her father and also saw Dr. Williams. This encounter was much calmer than that of the previous summer. Nonetheless, Lee Ann was upset for 10 days before the visit and for several weeks after. During the visit itself she had a sore throat. Her father got mad at her because he wanted Lee Ann to tell him she would rather be with him than with us. She refused. As Janet said, her honesty, which we all worked so hard to preserve, was not the most useful characteristic at that moment. Dr. Williams had been unable to work with Lee Ann's father because his father had become ill and he was very upset about that. Janet asked that one of us come and sit down with Dr. Williams and the staff at Neighborhood House to plan for the future. Paul went early in the fall.

They all agreed that it did not seem likely an early adoption could be worked out. Dr. Williams made several suggestions about things he felt we could do to celebrate Lee Ann's emotional bonding with the family—a kind of emotional adoption with a family party and a small gift. He also thought it would be better not to arrange visits with her father for a while. They were too upsetting to her. We needed to let Mr. Steinkohler decide his own degree of interest. Other than the visit arranged by Janet in the summer, we had had no contact with Mr. Steinkohler since the previous summer. The Neighborhood House staff felt that if it came to a case of custody, the agency could probably win, but not if we attempted adoption. We needed good legal help at home. Janet said she would come to our town and meet with Mrs. Brown so that everyone understood what was going on.

We found a new attorney who, at the suggestion of Neighborhood House, was of the majority political party and not involved in controversy. The County Welfare Department recommended him. The attorney said that when Lee Ann was 14 adoption would be easier, because her opinion would be taken into consideration. That did not seem right to us. We asked Mrs. Brown. She said we should ask a judge who hears such cases.

The judge reviewed our situation and said, "This is a case where justice and the law are not the same." Her father's mere appearance in court would decide the case in his favor. In adoptions, the biological parent's wishes overrode the stated best interest of the child. Our attorney had been thinking about custody in divorce cases.

Janet spent a day and a night with us. She liked Mrs. Brown and helped us straighten out this confusion about legal matters.

At about this time, Lee Ann began to experiment with new spellings of her name—first, Lee Anne, then Leighanne, and finally just Leigh. This new name seemed to go with a new identity, that of a more self-confident person.

In late August, we were glad to see Bill and Sarah return, after two years in Africa, with their newly adopted baby, Betsy. Sarah and I began to share care for our infants one morning a week, so Timothy had his first friend.

In the fall, it was time for seventh grade, and I felt panicky. How could Leigh be in junior high already? She needed more time to mature. There were many students at the junior high and some of them were bused in from rural areas. This was both a blessing and a disadvantage for Leigh. She made new friends who were from varied backgrounds, including a girl who lived on a farm with horses. But Leigh no longer had one teacher whom she knew well. It was a constant struggle to keep her from being tracked in school by evaluations that did not reflect her present growth.

Some class placements were made on the basis of tests given several years earlier. There were stimulating classes that we thought would interest Leigh, but they weren't open to her because of these test scores. We had to get special permission for her to take a particularly interesting English course. We worried that, because school personnel might lose track of Leigh's present development, decisions would be made that were not in her best interest. Again and again we had to tell the school to keep the options open and not to decide the future right away.

By now Stephen was three and a half years old and much pleased to have his own life. He was attending the preschool at the local college. Already I could feel that I was treated a little bit differently as Stephen's mother than I was as Leigh's. At Stephen's school, I was just a mom, and he was one of three Stephens in a group of 20 children. At Leigh's school, I was always having to explain who I was and who she was. By this time, with the advice of Dr. Williams, she was calling herself Leigh Lindsay, but she was still registered at school as Lee Ann Steinkohler.

Timothy began to walk and talk, and to reveal the vivid imagination behind those dark eyes. He liked animals, and tried to follow a rabbit to see where it lived. On a snowy day in February, we moved into our new house. Leigh loved going to school on the bus. Several friends lived in this neighborhood. She was no longer quiet or withdrawn, either at school or with friends. She was a petite, bubbly 13-year-old, often saying things that were very funny. She was the catcher at neighborhood baseball games, an expert horse rider, and a lover of every creature, from the guinea pigs she raised in her room to the snakes she and the boy next door caught in the woods.

Yet there were still things that worried us. She was sick a lot. Our doctor spent time with Leigh trying to figure out the connection between her emotional life and these physical illnesses. He thought that removing her tonsils might help. We had this done, but, unfortunately, in their place came new allergies. An allergist treated her with shots. The animals were so important to her that we tried to get by with keeping them. But we air-conditioned her room and removed the rug.

Sometimes, out of the blue, or so it seemed, things fell apart. One such time was a Sunday in early spring. Paul was usually gone almost all day on Sundays. Leigh was restless. There was nobody around to play with. She decided to ride her bicycle into town to visit the twins from our old neighborhood. She called and asked if she could stay for supper. I said no. I didn't have a car to pick her up and she needed to ride home before dark. I could tell from her voice that she was extremely annoyed, but it was out of character for her to disobey. Losing her home was too much of a real fear for her to threaten not to come home.

I put the boys to bed, and after I read to Stephen, I was surprised to see that it was completely dark and Leigh had still not returned. I called the twins' house. She had left for home, a 15-minute ride, an hour and a half before. I waited a few more minutes and called two or three friends in town she might have dropped in to see. No one had seen her.

I called Sarah, thinking Leigh might have come into the neighborhood and stopped to see her daughter Ruth. They had not seen her, but Sarah offered for Ruth to stay with the boys while she drove me into town to look for Leigh. We looked everywhere for the bicycle and realized that a kid who wanted to disappear could fade into any dorm or university building.

During the ride, Sarah said, "This is so upsetting. I keep thinking how I would feel if it were Ruth." I was overwhelmed with tears. This simple statement told me that she didn't consider herself as a mother or Ruth as a daughter any different from us. Until that moment, I didn't realize how seldom I had experienced this kind of acceptance as Leigh's mother.

We went home and Paul was there. Still no Leigh. Paul and Bill went out in the car to look for her. When they returned, just after we had called the police, Leigh walked through the door, scared and sobbing. She'd been angry when I told her to come home because she wanted to stay out later. After she left the twins' house, she'd stopped in to see two friends from school who I didn't know. They lived back in a little lane where we hadn't looked, and she'd put her bike on the porch out of sight. When she began to think of starting home, it was dark. Their mother was not at home, they had no telephone, and Leigh was scared. Finally, their mother came back and brought Leigh home. It became a larger event than she had intended.

I told Leigh that I didn't understand what had happened that evening and that I didn't think she did. I suggested that she write down her feelings about the day, and share them with us if she wanted to. When she came in from school the next day, she went to her room and began dutifully writing. An hour later she came into the kitchen and told me she didn't want to share her writing with me, but that she did have a better idea of what had happened.

She told me it was partly because of a movie she'd seen. I remembered that Leigh, her friend Judy, and I had gone to see a film about a boy and a girl being treated for emotional illnesses. They were living in a residential setting. Judy and I had discussed how moving the story was. At the time I had been surprised at Leigh's lack of response. Now Leigh told me that the setting had been so much like Neighborhood House that she felt mixed up, almost as if she was the girl in the movie. She had tried not to think about the film.

The next afternoon had been Sunday, and Paul was away at work. I had been too busy to talk. Judy had gone to a friend's house. Nobody had time for Leigh. She rode into town to the twins' house. They were not in a good mood, but they did finally invite her to stay for supper. After I refused permission to stay, she rode her bike by Paul's office. He was talking to someone, had his back to the door, and didn't see her. She felt abandoned. As she was riding home, she saw a boy from school and his sister, talked to them a while, and went to their house. Finally, their mother brought her home. The feelings she'd had all that Sunday were pretty scary.

I told her that I was glad she understood her feelings better. I said I was sorry we hadn't talked on Sunday, and that I understood how feelings from the past catch up with us and events get bigger than we intend sometimes. I also emphasized how important it is to be honest about plans and that she had to inform us if there was a change of plans.

I had scary feelings too. I was afraid that the combination of the mood swings of adolescence and all the past feelings of abandonment and uncertainty would be so painful that Leigh would try to avoid feeling them by choosing the wrong friends or by withdrawing into depression or illness.

The following fall, when Leigh was in eighth grade, we spent Thanksgiving with Paul's parents. They enjoyed the children, and took care of Timothy one day while we took Leigh and Stephen into the city. Everyone was still caught up in reaction to the assassination of President Kennedy a few days before. We were especially glad that we made this trip, because Paul's father died unexpectedly and suddenly of an aneurysm two months later. Leigh's grandfather died a few days after that. She didn't attend either service, partly because she was recovering from flu at the time. Dr. Williams said, "Don't send her." Leigh said, "Don't make me go. It would be too scary." We sent a note and flowers from us and from her. The silence from Leigh's father continued.

The civil rights movement continued to be part of our lives. In the summer of 1964, training sessions for the Mississippi Freedom Summer were held at our local college. In early June, one group had already gone to Mississippi, and the whole country knew that three of them were missing. The second group felt tense as they boarded the buses for Mississippi. They accidentally jostled some wedding guests in the college parking lot. For some local citizens, this was a serious lack of good manners and civility. The town was deeply divided by the presence of these long-haired, barefoot, idealistic students, and the issues they raised caused deep rifts within the community. For the first time, beliefs taken for granted were being called into question.

At the end of June, Paul and Gail answered an appeal for white ministers to help in a protest in Birmingham, Alabama, so that blacks would not give up on an integrated civil rights movement. They stayed and walked in picket lines for a week. Leigh and I went down on the weekend. Leigh was impressed by the emotion of a mass meeting, and moved by the warm welcome she received. We ate in the homes of movement members and met students at Miles College, where we stayed. On July 4th, the day the new public accommodations bill became law, we ate with a black civil rights leader and his family at the Holiday Inn.

Friends wondered why we took Leigh with us. There were three reasons. I didn't know if the student couple who had agreed to stay with the little boys could handle the teenage neighborhood scene at our house that summer. We also felt this was an important part of the history of our time. And it was an opportunity for Leigh to meet people who had serious problems and were dealing with them in courageous ways. We found all these things and more.

In the middle of our time in Birmingham, to get a break, we went to see the Beatles' film *A Hard Day's Night,* our first experience of their music. The Beatles' songs became intermingled in my memories of that tumultuous summer. Leigh was invited to go to a Beatles concert in a nearby city a few weeks later. She carefully picked out the songs she thought Paul would like so she could share them with him. They bought a guitar and both took lessons.

Life was very different for us now than in the first few years Leigh was with us. The large problems were still there, but they were no longer the only or even the central things in her life. She was very much the teenage girl, enthusiastically developing new interests and thinking about the future. Animals were still important, along with painting, drawing, clothes, decorating, cooking, and sports. Music was something she enjoyed and continued to share with Paul. He appreciated this because it helped him to know what his students were listening to.

It had been a long time since we'd heard from Mr. Steinkohler. It seemed unlikely now that he would seriously try to have Leigh removed from our home. She was happy and productive more of the time, but the deeply upsetting periods never completely disappeared. When she felt such despair, we worried about the past overwhelming her. We still saw the possibility of her retreating into some kind of depression, and that worried us.

When we took the students on their workcamp in the spring, something new was happening. We observed one of the pilot programs for Head Start, an effort to help disadvantaged preschool children. I visited the classes of small children, who, along with their families, were being helped to learn and have good health. I connected instantly with this idea. What a great help that kind of program would have been for Leigh, even if everything else had been the same. It seemed a way to change the direction of children's lives for the better, and we went home talking about it.

We found out that the Head Start program was going to be expanded for the summer. Getting together a committee from our community, a friend and I organized the writing of a grant proposal for Head Start. The two lab school directors wrote the education program. A sociologist let us use a study he had done of the county to demonstrate the need. The school system loaned typing time.

After we mailed the proposal, I would wake up in the night, fearful that all the volunteers my proposal depended on would not materialize. The grant was approved. The program sparked the imagination of people looking for meaningful ways to help. We had volunteer classroom helpers, drivers, and office workers. My contribution at this point was to contact and involve the parents. This was similar to what I had done in our group ministry, and I enjoyed it. I also helped mediate between the principal of the school building we were using and the lab school teacher who was organizing the program.

At one point I thought the whole program would go down the drain over the issue of tricycles. The principal said, "I can't have black tire marks on the floor." The lab school teacher said, "We can't have a classroom for threes and fours without tricycles." After long discussion, we compromised. We used tricycles, and we cleaned off the minor tracks. We had a good program, and I was pleased at the thought of all the children like Leigh who were being helped.

After the summer was well underway, we went to the island off the coast of North Carolina that we liked so much, renting a very simple cabin for a month. Leigh rented a horse named Bud for a couple of dollars a day. The boys played pirates in the coves where Blackbeard had hidden booty. That same summer we visited Williamsburg, Virginia, where a colonial village has been recreated. Leigh was completely absorbed in the atmosphere. She wanted to know everything about the people who had once lived there and their way of life. The boys were playing the radio in the car, and she said, "Turn that off. I'm in love with the eighteenth century."

When we came back from summer vacation, Leigh was excited about being in ninth grade, the first year of high school. Her friends from junior high would all be there, and there were many more people to meet. She was, at fourteen and a half, not quite five feet tall. She wore her long brown hair in the current style, with bangs obscuring her eyebrows. She dressed in saucy short skirts and sweaters and was always neat as a pin. She was lively, interested in just about everything, and still said very humorous things. She was fun to be with, and most of the time she was very involved with animals and people.

When she wasn't smiling, there was a sadness in her eyes, and there were still times when she sat silently within a group without being a part of it. It was impossible at those times for me to know what she was thinking.

On the plus side, I could see clearly the benefits of the extra sixth grade year. Both Leigh's academic skills and her social relationships were comparable to those of others her age.

In many ways, the first three years of high school were years of steady growth in a variety of directions. Leigh's confidence with people increased by leaps and bounds. She had friends from the neighborhood. I don't think she always felt unconditional acceptance, but she was a part of the group. She had also made a number of friends from all over our one-hundred-square-mile school district. When she learned to drive, and we drove to a nearby town, I sometimes thought she knew every second car on the road.

Her appreciation of adults was still a delightful part of who she was. Once, a prominent writer on civil rights, John Howard Griffin, spoke on the campus. Leigh had read his book, *Black Like Me,* and she went to hear him speak. After his talk Paul invited him to our house to eat. When I came in from taking the baby-sitter home, Leigh was sitting in the living room in her pajamas, comfortably discussing the racial problems at her high school with this very sophisticated man. She had put him completely at ease.

In 1965, when Leigh was 15, Janet wrote to say that Doris, the director of Neighborhood House, was retiring. She and Janet were both moving to London. The agency would be able to help us if we needed them, but they had changed their focus some time earlier to become a residential center for emotionally disturbed children. Janet told us that a law had passed in that state saying that if a child had been in one foster home for 10 years and was also 18 years old, she could make her own decision about adoption. She pointed out that this would be Leigh's situation on her 18th birthday. We were sorry to learn they were leaving, and felt a little uneasy, but we had developed a good relationship with Mrs. Brown and knew she was well informed about our situation.

We had not heard from Leigh's father at all for about a year after his father died. Then we received a letter in an entirely new voice. We had no idea who was writing for him. It was a pleasant, friendly letter, which we answered, telling him about Leigh's current life.

In another six weeks we received another letter informing us that Mr. Steinkohler had married. He told us his wife's name. Leigh recognized her as the oldest daughter in her first foster home, and she was very upset by this news. She was afraid that he would want her to come live with him now. In addition, she remembered this young woman as being very mean to her. Leigh became angry about little things that usually didn't bother her—her brothers' noise, remarks by friends, ingredients missing in the kitchen. She spent more time alone listening to music in her room.

We got a letter every few weeks for some time, which we answered with newsy reports of Leigh's life. Finally, one announced the birth of a son. Each letter was upsetting to Leigh, but they never seemed to really threaten her.

That year, when Leigh was 15, she registered for a month-long summer camp in New Hampshire. She was looking forward to it. In the spring, a letter came from her father saying that he and his family would like to visit us in July. That was our vacation month, as well as Leigh's time to be at camp. We wrote to ask if they could come in June or August, since we would not be home in July. There was no reply.

I wrote again and explained we would be away the entire month of July. I wrote again, and still there was no reply. I called Neighborhood House and asked them to relay the message. Then I talked to Mrs. Brown, who said, "Go on and go. Don't tell anyone in the neighborhood where you're going." (We always had some fear of having to deal with Mr. Steinkohler on unfamiliar ground.) We wrote one last time in vain.

About the first of July, we left to take Leigh to camp, to visit Paul's family on the way, and to camp at Mount Desert Island with the boys and visit Sarah and Bill at their cabin on an island in Maine.

Leigh had a wonderful experience at camp. She said it was the best time she ever had. Some other girls in her tent were adopted. The counselor was wonderful. They planned their whole day, except for swimming, and together they went on several two- or three-day hikes. It was good for Leigh to have a positive experience away from home.

When we arrived home in August, we found a blistering letter from Leigh's father. They had driven 600 miles to our house in July and we were not there. The letter contained negative descriptions of the neighbors on the left and on the right. Each of the neighbors also had their own descriptions of Mr. Steinkohler and his wife.

We wrote and told Mr. Steinkohler that we were sorry they had come when we weren't home, and that we did not know why they didn't understand we were going to be away. We continued to receive letters, sometimes friendly, sometimes angry, and two announcing the birth of another baby.

The next fall, in tenth grade, Leigh began to date a classmate named Matt who lived on a farm about five miles away. She liked the rural lifestyle and the animals. Matt's father had died several years before. He seemed to enjoy our family life, and Paul was a father figure for him.

I worried about the amount of time Leigh and Matt spent together. Leigh was not meeting a variety of boys, and Matt seemed to stifle her growth with his narrow perspectives. I worried that the relationship would be too serious too soon. He was a committed member of a fundamentalist church, which did not permit dancing. Leigh loved music and dancing. I hated for her to miss these kinds of school events. (Finally, the year of Leigh's senior prom, he decided it would be OK to go.) They did have a different kind of fun—making pizza, riding horses, and spending lots of time at our house. He liked to shoot baskets with Stephen.

The summer Leigh was 16 we went on a camping trip to Florida. My parents went too, and invited Leigh to stay with them in a hotel on the beach. She spent almost all her time missing Matt and being perfectly put together. She had to iron her shorts to go out to the fishing pier in the rain to pick up Stephen and Timothy. She hardly opened her curtains to look at the ocean. My dad allowed her to make telephone calls to Matt, and I was unhappy with both my dad and Leigh about all those phone calls. I wondered where our outdoor girl had gone. She decided to go home with Granddaddy and Nanna when they were ready to leave before we were. She said, "They understand me." I was glad Leigh had a good relationship with them at a time when it was hard for her to be comfortable with me.

Her best academic experiences were in summer school, where there was no ability grouping, classes were small, and students studied together in the afternoons. She enjoyed this ambiance and learned easily. In an oil painting class at the university she discovered a real gift for composition, and her teacher recognized her artistic ability. Though she did not continue, this skill was one more thing she could pick up later on to add richness to her life.

The fall of Leigh's junior year, a French-speaking cousin of Paul's from Belgium came to stay with us for the school year. Marie went to our local college. Although the girls were very different, it was a good experience for both of them. Marie spent her first night in the Midwest at the county fair with Leigh and Matt, waiting for Matt's pigs to be born. Leigh learned about a person from a different culture with a different educational experience and found some common ground with her.

In school during this time, Leigh's development was uneven. In most ways she could do as well as her classmates, but in some ways she still needed special help. The role I played with the school was mostly to remind her teachers, in a paraphrase of a teenage poster, "Please remember that she's not finished yet." She still needed an advocate. School rules prohibited her from taking a French class because her English grade had not been high enough. I explained to the principal that we had a French-speaking young person living with us, how Leigh's English could improve with study of a foreign language, and that Marie's help would be a motivating factor. Finally, they allowed her to sign up, and she became an excellent French student.

Leigh's high school years were a confusing time for us and I am sure for Leigh as well. Though she still had neighborhood friends, increasingly her time was spent with friends from the country whose families had different expectations, life-styles, and social values. In those families, the roles of men and women were traditional, and education for women was not considered important. There was only one role for a woman: that of wife and mother. There was little emphasis on individual growth. With my own emphasis on equality of men and women and the importance of growth for both boys and girls, I felt that this traditional view was not helpful.

One friend of Leigh's we had known since seventh grade, when she was a bareback-riding lively tomboy who read horse stories and wrote them as well. She was bright and fun to be with, and over the years I spent a lot of time talking with her and listening to her. She asked good, searching questions and had lots of ability. At graduation we were all invited to a party at her house. She was the first member of her family ever to graduate from high school. The graduation gifts looked like presents for a bridal shower to me: lingerie and household objects. The mother had five children. Leigh's friend was somewhere in the middle. A slightly older daughter, who had been pregnant at 16, had her two children in tow. The mother kept a spotless house and took lots of "nerve medicine," which seemed to cover everything from menopause to depression. She and the older daughter told gory stories about childbirth. Since at that point I'd had no experience with childbirth, my opinion was of little value.

I had never expected to have such strong feelings about cultural differences. Most of my life, I had refused to judge people on the basis of money or name. I felt uncomfortable with people in our university town who based their judgments about others on degrees, grades, or books they'd published. I found Leigh's friends and some of their parents interesting people. I encouraged Leigh to be open to varied personalities, and I valued her ability to choose people to trust one by one. What bothered me about the girls' and Matt's families was that they saw only one "right" way to grow up. The hard work we had done to encourage Leigh to consider many options seemed to be getting lost.

I worried that if she tried too hard to fit into a narrow definition of herself she would lose the very things that were her survival skills—her questions, her anger, her honesty. And I still worried that the many losses in her life, which always had to be worked through whenever she faced a new crisis, would be so overwhelming that she would deny them and withdraw.

Most of our interaction as mother and daughter, however, was on a much more mundane level. Leigh and I had running battles over the toys the boys left scattered in the playroom and the short amount of time I spent with the vacuum cleaner. I offered her the opportunity to make it better, and actually she did help a lot, but household perfection was not a high priority for me.

She brought her friends home, and they hung around discussing movies or boyfriends or homework assignments while I worked in the kitchen. One day I told her, "You said last week that your friends like to come here because I listen. Well, if the vacuum cleaner was always running, I wouldn't be able to hear them!"

It was very hard for me to know what Leigh really wanted for herself for the future. Certainly at that time she was looking for simple answers, and her friends' families seemed to have them.

They also had very different political views from ours. I remember an afternoon in 1965, around the time of the march from Selma to Montgomery, less than a year after our trip to Birmingham. The whole country was absorbed in the debate about voting rights. Leigh came in from the school bus with a scowl on her face, and said, "Discrimination against Negroes doesn't exist. They could vote if they really wanted to. Everybody says that."

I knew she must have heard this from one of her classmates. I asked her if she thought that the minister we met in Birmingham wasn't telling the truth, and I gave her some reports he'd written about police brutality. For a long time she held conflicting ideas without resolving the inconsistencies. She was not interested in local issues, but watched, with great emotion, the civil rights events on television. Sometimes the speakers were people we had met in Birmingham.

During Leigh's junior year, opposition to the Vietnam war grew. The son of a campus ministry colleague had refused to register for the draft, and he was being tried in a federal court in Cincinnati, with much publicity. He was someone our children all knew, who lived in our neighborhood and had shared many family meals with us. Leigh was conflicted over the issue. Matt's mother kept sending tracts about the war being a Christian Crusade. Some people in Leigh's school, teachers as well as students, thought people who opposed the war were unpatriotic or even subversive. Paul was doing draft counseling with students, and his views were an embarrassment to Leigh.

One night she and Matt arrived at our house. Leigh looked pale, and Matt told us, "That draft dodger really got it this time." They had heard the announcement on the car radio that our friend had been convicted and sentenced to three years in prison. After Matt left, Leigh sat down and tearfully told us how hard it was when people she liked disagreed. On the one hand she wanted to believe the war was right, and her friends all thought it was. On the other hand, she knew the convicted man and knew he wasn't the terrible person the radio described.

Over time all of our children have had these kinds of experiences, testing their own or their family's values against values of friends and community, and trying out different ways of thinking and being. It was never our goal to have any of them parrot our views, but rather to share our ideas and ideals as one part of what they put together to develop their own. The thing that was different with Leigh was that she was still working hard on the most basic parts of her identity.

Was she a member of this family or not? What were her early values, and how did that affect her now? At a time when it is appropriate to rebel, she wasn't sure she was secure enough in her relationahips to rebel safely. This led to great confusion and unpredictable responses. Sometimes she expressed diametrically opposed ideas. Sometimes she dogmatically accepted simplistic answers.

What we tried to do with Leigh as well as the others was to hold up a mirror of the positive traits we knew she had, even though they were not obviously present at the time. We tried to communicate our awareness of this "hidden self" by pointing out those traits whenever we could.

Occasionally, there were blocks of time for discussion away from the interruptions of daily life, such as camping trips, restaurant meals, or a long ride to the mall with a single child. Once, when Leigh was having problems with conflicting ideas about the war, Paul got permission for her to miss a day of school so she could accompany him to pick up a nationally known speaker at a college across the state. It gave Leigh time to talk with Paul on the way and time on the way back to meet an interesting person. She wrote a paper on his ideas about the war.

During the spring of Leigh's junior year, much to my amazement and excitement, I found out I was pregnant. The baby was due in November. I was concerned about how the other children would feel. I thought Leigh might be embarrassed. We decided to involve them all as much as possible. The doctor was an infertility specialist I had seen for years and used as a gynecologist even after he said there was no more he could do. He was very excited, but apprehensive. He suggested I drive once a month to see him and, other than that, that I stay home.

Leigh reacted with excitement. The boys were interested and thought a baby would be great. The pregnancy was a good experience for all of them, and turned out to be normal in every way. We took natural childbirth classes, the Lamaze method arriving halfway through. The doctor arranged for Paul to be in the delivery room.

Meanwhile, Leigh became anxious to make her adoption final "before I graduate next June." We knew that, according to Janet's statement, we could do this in January, because Leigh would be 18 then. It would have to be done in the court in her father's county. Leigh found that prospect scary.

There was no such law in our state, but we thought we could get her father or the court to agree to the adoption if the new law was known to them. We hired a new attorney, a man we knew and respected. When we told him the history, he assured us he could work it out. I don't think at that time he really believed all we told him about our experiences with Leigh's father.

Leigh had been looking forward to a trip to the World's Fair in Canada. When I couldn't go, Paul decided she could invite a friend. He also arranged to take Stephen to Chicago and Timothy to a closer city overnight, so that each of them could also have a special time with him. We told Mr. Stewart, the attorney, to wait until they came back from Canada before sending the papers. Just about the same time, we got a letter from Leigh's father saying they would like to visit us on a certain date in August. We had not heard from them in almost a year. We wrote back: "Please come. We'll be expecting you." We told Mr. Stewart, again, to wait until we talked to Leigh's father when they came.

I wrote again about two weeks before they were to come to tell them we were looking forward to their visit. Timothy, who was five, was just beginning to understand the word *adoption*. It seemed there was a lot going on that could confuse him. Bill and Sarah, who had moved an hour away, invited him to spend the weekend of Leigh's father's visit. Our friend Pamela, who was both a social worker and an adoptive parent, was standing by for Stephen. Other friends and neighbors were on the alert to help in case of emergency.

The time came for the visit. We waited all weekend, with Leigh becoming more and more upset. They sent no message, but they never came. We told Mr. Stewart to wait until we could find out what happened. It was a couple of weeks before we received a letter saying something had come up, so they had decided not to come.

We called Mr. Stewart to go ahead with the legal proceedings for adoption. We wanted to complete the adoption before the baby arrived.

When Mr. Steinkohler was informed of the adoption hearing, he wrote us an angry letter. Mr. Stewart called to say that Mr. Steinkohler had hired an attorney and planned to come to our county court to contest the adoption.

Leigh was 17 and a high school senior. School had just begun, and she was having all manner of trouble. She could not concentrate. Early one rainy evening that September, Leigh asked if she could borrow the car to take her typewriter to a friend who lived on a farm out in the county. I told her to be careful on the rain-slick road, and she said she would be back before dark.

I was especially tired. I cleared the dishes from the table and sat down to visit with Paul. I told him I didn't think I could handle one more thing that day, and started to describe my busy day. In the background, we heard a siren going into town from the nearby highway. A few minutes later the phone rang and the voice on the other end told us there had been an accident, that Leigh was at the hospital emergency room, that she was conscious and was being treated.

Paul hung up the phone. We called a close friend to come stay with the boys while we went to the hospital. When we arrived the ambulance driver was waiting for us at the door. He was a man I knew. I had worked on a committee with the League of Women Voters about city workers' salaries, and he had appreciated this. He told us that he was the one who had gone to help our daughter. He thought she was all right. He had waited to tell us that she was worried about me. "She said that you are expecting a very special baby, and she wanted me to tell you not to be upset."

Leigh was not hurt. They kept her at the hospital because she was so shaken up. A doctor came in and questioned me as to what the hidden things were. He said she was more upset than the situation warranted.

"Did she take the car without permission? Did you have an argument?" "No, no," I said. "We are in the midst of an adoption case. I think that has something to do with it." The car was totaled. She had hit a tree at a curve on the rain-slick road.

After the accident, Leigh was so depressed and withdrawn she couldn't go to school for a week. She sat in her room all day and stared out the window. She didn't call her friends or participate with the family. She just sat. I was completely worn out with worry. It felt like she was going to fall apart completely. When she had been home from the hospital three days, she finally agreed to see a psychologist with whom we had worked in Head Start. She saw him once and he helped her deal with the emergency. When she came home, she wanted to call Dr. Williams, and they talked for a long time. Then he asked to speak to me.

"I told her I have no magic in an hour, but if she still feels she wants to come, I've saved one o'clock on Friday for her. I think she needs to see and think about who Lee Ann Steinkohler was before she can see who Leigh Lindsay might be."

We called Neighborhood House. A social worker there said he would make arrangements for her to stay at a nearby Holiday Inn and would also meet her at the airport.

The day before she left was September 27, Timothy's sixth birthday. We had, two weeks before, invited his friends for a party with a circus theme. Stephen and his friend Dan were going to dress up like clowns. It seemed important to keep something normal. Leigh offered to bake the cupcakes. She wanted to do this for Timothy. It was the only break from complete depression we had seen since the accident. The whole house had a smell of cherry cake. Somehow we had the party, and Timothy had a good time.

Our hearts were heavy as we drove Leigh to the airport the next day. There was a feeling of separation, of her leaving emotionally in a very different way. I hugged her at the gate and went back to the car and cried and cried. I worried about the baby. I was glad that we were only a month and a half from the due date and that so far the pregnancy had been very normal.

Leigh called on Friday evening. The social worker had taken her to the appointment with Dr. Williams. After a long talk, Dr. Williams had decided she needed to see her father. Dr. Williams and the social worker took her to her father's house, where she talked with him and his wife and met and played with the children.

She told us she was feeling confused. She didn't know what she wanted to do. She missed all of us and loved us, but maybe it wasn't a good time for the adoption. I told her that whatever she decided was what we should do.

Mr. Stewart had called earlier in the day. He had been talking to Mr. Steinkohler's attorney. The attorney had tried to convince Mr. Steinkohler that it would be very expensive and painful to contest the adoption, and that it was unlikely that he could win. Pursuing this was not in his best interest.

We picked Leigh up at the airport. She still seemed shaken and was very quiet on the trip home. Later in the evening she came into our room to talk. She said, "My father gave me his telephone number. It's unlisted, you know. They came to see me at the motel late last night. At first, I was scared, but they came to tell me they want me to be happy. If adoption is what I want, it's OK. I feel so strange. Those children are so different from Stephen and Timothy. They get yelled at. There's not much to play with. I almost couldn't stand it. I don't know what to do."

Paul told her, "There is no rush. Wait till you know what you want." We called Mr. Stewart, explained the situation, and told him to put everything on hold.

Unfortunately, Matt had been frightened by Leigh's behavior and her depression. He stayed away from our house and did not call her. Leigh cried and raged.

Leigh went back to school the Monday after she returned on Saturday. She was overwhelmed by the academic program she had been taking, so she switched to a new course in which she worked part time selling toys at a local store. She liked the people she worked with and they liked her, and the customers thought she was special.

Several days later she came home with a cardboard box of crayons, paints, paper, and small toys that represented her whole week's wages. "These are for my father's children. He and his wife really don't know what to buy for them. Will you help me mail this box?" We carefully packed it and she took it to the post office.

Leigh was making new friends in her class. They came home with her to work on projects. She was still very upset, but she was reaching out to other students and was beginning to have a little fun. Her heavy mood was beginning to lift.

Mr. Stewart called. Mr. Steinkohler's attorney had told him that Mr. Steinkohler had decided not to contest the adoption. We told Leigh this, but we assured her that whatever she decided was OK. The hearing was scheduled for October 13. Mr. Stewart said he was holding this date, but it could be continued or canceled. Several days later Leigh decided to go ahead with the adoption.

Mr. Stewart talked with Mr. Steinkohler's attorney. Together, they called Leigh's father to make sure he still agreed to the adoption. He still did.

On the afternoon of the adoption hearing, we picked up Leigh and Stephen at school. Timothy brought a bag of toys in case there was a long wait. The boys were excited, giggling and moving about in the car. Leigh sat beside them, silent and uninvolved, her thoughts inscrutable to me. Timothy said, "We're going to get Leigh registered, right?" I reminded him that what we were doing was called *adoption*, that we would talk to a judge, and that the judge would write down in his book that Leigh would be forever part of the Lindsay family, just as we thought she had been for a long time.

When we went into the court building, Mr. Stewart was waiting for us. There was a drink machine in sight, and of course, everyone was thirsty. With drinks in hand, Timothy spread out his collection of toys and he and Stephen began to play. Leigh still sat in silence. Almost immediately a secretary came to tell us that the judge was waiting in his office.

The judge's office was a wood-paneled room with a large desk, a small couch, and several comfortable chairs. The same friendly, gentle man who had given us advice several years before sat behind it. He greeted us and spoke to each of the children. Then Mr. Stewart and I both realized that the boys still had their drinks and Timothy was trailing his toys behind him. We collected these things, and I explained to the boys that this was a serious place and a special time. We all sat down.

The judge said he had studied the case carefully and everything seemed to be in order. He would need no further evidence. He suggested that we give Mr. Steinkohler a chance to sign the adoption papers voluntarily, so that no statement of neglect would have to be part of the proceeding. That was fine with us.

Leigh spoke for the first time. "I don't understand. Am I adopted or not? What I mean is: Is it OK to have the party?"

The judge said, "Yes, by all means, have the party. You are going to be adopted."

In a burst of relief and conversation, Leigh began to tell him how we were going to our favorite restaurant and we were even going to have a special cake. He smiled and said, "Go, and enjoy it very much, Miss Lindsay."

After so many years of waiting, it was over in less than 15 minutes. The hearing was anticlimactic, but the party wasn't. The little Italian restaurant was festive with its all-the-time Christmas lights, bright pictures, hanging bottles and baskets, and red and white checked tablecloths. We ordered the pizza, with various combinations of ingredients, and by luck, a jovial and most attentive waitress served us. Timothy asked her for more cola, and when she brought it, he said, "She brings me anything I ask for. I wish she was my mother!"

Leigh's eyes were bright as she talked happily about the future and about this day. "I really am a Lindsay now!" We handed her our gift, three yards of Lindsay plaid wool fabric from Scotland and a special charm on a chain, made by a friend, of a small human figure with arms outstretched, called "So Big." The day had a complete and very calm feeling.

The papers were sent to Mr. Steinkohler to sign. Two weeks and three weeks went by, but no papers were returned. Mr. Stewart and Mr. Steinkohler's attorney tried to call again, but the unlisted number had been changed. The judge said, "This is just too much. This adoption is final!"

The bill we received from Mr. Stewart did not reflect the number of hours we knew he had spent on this case. When we called to check on this, he replied, "I've been more than well paid. My son met Leigh at a party. She asked if he were my son. Then she said, 'Tell your father that I love him.'"

On November 4, Susan Carol Lindsay was born. The hospital, at the last minute, had changed the rules, so that no fathers were allowed in the delivery room. Paul called to complain. The nun who was the head administrator said, "Mr. Lindsay, slow down. I agree with you. I'm going by the old rules, if your doctor approves." So Paul and I experienced this truly miraculous event together.

My mother had planned to be with us, but she had had a heart attack in August. We were worried about her constantly, with my doctor following each day's progress to help me to decide if I should risk going to see her. She was much better now, but not yet well enough to join us.

Leigh was still picking up the pieces of her life, and she was not completely stabilized. She complained about the boys' noise, often went right to her room when she came in from work, and was upset if the washing machine wasn't readily available. I didn't want the tension of depending on any help from her at this time. So she worked after school and I hired two home economics majors from the university to alternate doing housework and taking care of the boys after school for a couple of weeks.

The final episode in the adoption was a letter Leigh received from Mr. Steinkohler's wife at Thanksgiving. She said that she hoped Leigh was happy. They had had nothing to eat at Thanksgiving, because Mr. Steinkohler was so upset about the adoption that he could not work. She went on to say, "What he gave you was not money but love."

Leigh was devastated by this letter. But fortunately, it was so extreme that it was fairly easy for her to see that it was overstated. I told her, "Any problems your father may have are not your fault. We both know he did the best he could, but it is hard to recognize his kind of love."

In January we received a cheery, newsy letter, just as if nothing had happened in the fall.

One of the things that always helped Leigh cope was her ability to see the funny aspects of an unpleasant event. One day she and I were shopping. Susan was with us in her stroller. The former Girl Scout leader who had caused so much frustration for Leigh in the sixth grade came up to us and saw Susan. "I didn't know you finally had a child," she remarked to me. As she walked away, I was feeling a little nonplussed.

Leigh said, "Don't worry about it, Mom. What we should have said was, 'Oh, this isn't a new child. This is Leigh. She didn't grow after she met you!'"

Matt and Leigh got back together, first with sporadic telephone calls and many apologies, then occasional dates, and finally, things were just as they had always been. On Valentine's Day she had a ring. She said, "Mom, you don't seem happy. Everyone else is happy for me."

I said, "Leigh, do you want me to lie? I'm really worried about a lot of things." Paul and I asked Leigh and Matt to come talk with us. We told them we were worried about their youth. We worried about Matt's religious beliefs and how that would affect birth control. We thought it would be overwhelming for Leigh to have too many children or too soon. We worried about his beliefs and psychotherapy, if Leigh should need help again. They listened, and Matt said he understood the importance of these things. Both thought their youth was not a problem. They knew what they wanted. They agreed to wait a year. Matt was going into the National Guard and Leigh needed some job training.

Neither Leigh nor Matt had finished growing emotionally or determining their interests. Leigh still reacted to negative experiences with the old feeling of "Nothing good happens to me." She still interpreted conflicts or even casual comments from people at work or at school as confirmation of her failure and lack of acceptance. Both Leigh and Matt were insecure. Marriage offered an alternative to the hard task of working through their insecure feelings to become strong individuals. Each thought the other would take care of him or her and together they would face the world.

Leigh was insecure for the obvious reason of her difficult childhood. She now had a group of lively friends and interesting activities, a job she liked, and people who cared a lot about her. But this was not enough to erase past feelings of exclusion. For Matt, the problems had begun with his father's death when he was 12. Growing up on a farm, with all its extra responsibilities, and having to work as well made it difficult for him to participate in high school activities. He didn't get enough help and encouragement to feel academically successful. His older brother, who he depended upon, had been in Vietnam, and had just returned much changed by the experience.

With the decision to marry, difficult educational and vocational decisions became less important to Leigh. The reality was that Leigh's academic progress during high school offered her the opportunity for college. But her negative feelings about her frustrating school years still persisted, and she did not want to try college. After she graduated from high school, she worked at the toy store over the summer and took an airline reservations training course in the fall. She took a job in a local travel agency and used her work experience well. Through traveling and relating to clients, she learned about the world, and her self-confidence grew.

By the next spring, we were still worried about the approaching marriage. But it was very clear we could not do much about it. So we gave Leigh and Matt as much emotional support as we could.

People who had been important to Leigh were making big efforts to be with her for the wedding. Bob and Jean were coming from Cleveland and Sarah and Bill from West Virginia. My sister, who had a real fear of flying, was going to take off and land five times between Raleigh-Durham and our airport. Paul's mother from New Jersey and her sister from New Mexico would be there. My mother had a new dress, and we talked each day on the phone. She wanted so much to come, and Leigh wanted her to be there. Finally, we decided the risk was too great.

There were teachers, counselors, employers, and, of course, the neighborhood children, her brothers and their friends. Matt thought she should invite her father. We told Leigh she was the one who should decide. She was too scared, and felt his presence would ruin the day for her.

On the day the out-of-town guests were arriving, the mail brought a letter from Mr. Steinkohler's wife. It began, "I'm writing you because you're the only person who would understand." It went on to tell me about problems in the family, that she felt she had to leave her husband, and that she was pregnant with a fourth child. She said she wanted to send the three children to me, since I had done such a good job with Lee Ann!

I got on the phone with Pamela, my good friend who was a social worker. "You offered to help with the wedding. I've got a strange request. Can you find me a social worker with a calm, warm, accepting voice? Tell her the brief outline of this, and get her phone number."

Pamela did. I wrote a letter telling Mrs. Steinkohler that my situation had changed. I now had four children. Her children needed to stay with her. Lee Ann's life had not been easy. The social worker whose number I was sending would help her keep her family together and help her to get job training. I wished her well.

The wedding turned out to be entirely different from what I had expected. I had thought it would be a warm gathering of family and friends, and it was. But I had worried, and so had Leigh, that the many different lifestyles would collide. That didn't happen. There was a wonderful feeling of mutual support. On a stormy June night we gathered in the university chapel decorated with candles and flowers. Timothy and Stephen lighted the candles. A traditional organ processional and a beautiful solo voice singing Leonard Bernstein's "One Hand, One Heart" filled the chapel. I sat quietly in my row, and although no less worried about the marriage, I was overcome with the feeling that this was a celebration of Lee Ann-Leigh's life and a coming of age.

The next morning my sister said, "I'm glad Mother didn't come, but for none of the reasons we talked about. For those of us who have known Leigh since she was eight, the experience was so emotionally overwhelming that I am not sure it would have been good for Mother."

I knew what she meant. I had turned to watch Leigh in her traditional satin dress walk down the aisle on Paul's arm. Her steps were uncertain at first, but then there was a broad smile to all of her friends and relatives and confidence increasing with each step. I felt as if she were saying to us all, "I'm going to be me. I'm going to take a chance on life."

Epilogue

I would like to write, as the fairy tales say, that they lived happily ever after. But we all know that isn't true. The marriage lasted about six years, ending because the partners had grown in vastly different directions.

Leigh was working for a travel agency and remained single for a couple of years until she met her present husband. They have a daughter who is the light of their life and brightens ours as well. It is truly a joy to watch Leigh parent so well, and in some ways, to redeem the past.

But life has also brought huge losses: two miscarriages before the healthy baby daughter, and a husband's battles with cancer.

In each of these events the terrible sadness of the past needed to be dealt with, as well as the event itself.

There are many parts of Leigh now. The frightened and angry little girl is there, but so is the "good enough mother," the loyal friend, the competent scout leader, the understanding and creative preschool teacher, the caring wife, and, most of all, the Leigh who takes care of herself.

About the Author

Caroline Hassinger Lindsay, an educator, has taught at Epworth Pre-School in Durham, North Carolina, for 20 years. She has a bachelor's degree from the University of North Carolina at Chapel Hill and a master's degree from Columbia Teacher's College and Union Theological Seminary in New York City.

The mother of four children, three of whom are adopted, including "Leigh," she facilitates workshops for parents and teachers. She lives in Chapel Hill, North Carolina, with her husband Paul.